The Productive
WRITER

TIPS & TOOLS TO HELP YOU **WRITE MORE,** STRESS LESS & **CREATE SUCCESS**

WD

WRITER'S DIGEST
BOOKS

WritersDigest.com
Cincinnati, Ohio

SAGE COHEN

For more resources for writers, visit www.writersdigest.com/books.

To receive a free weekly e-mail newsletter delivering tips and updates about writing and about Writer's Digest products, register directly at http://newsletters.fwpublications.com.

14 13 12 11 10   5 4 3 2 1

Distributed in Canada by Fraser Direct, 100 Armstrong Avenue, Georgetown, Ontario, Canada L7G 5S4, Tel: (905) 877-4411. Distributed in the U.K. and Europe by F+W Media International, Brunel House, Newton Abbot, Devon, TQ12 4PU, England, Tel: (+44) 1626-323200, Fax: (+44) 1626-323319, E-mail: postmaster@davidandcharles.co.uk. Distributed in Australia by Capricorn Link, P.O. Box 704, Windsor, NSW 2756 Australia, Tel: (02) 4577-3555.

Library of Congress Cataloging-in-Publication Data

Cohen, Sage.

   The productive writer : tips & tools to help you write more, stress less, & create success / by Sage Cohen.

      p. cm.

   ISBN 978-1-58297-995-3 (alk. paper)

   1. Authorship--Handbooks, manuals, etc. I. Title.

   PN147.C725 2010

   808'.02--dc22

                              2010028411

Edited by Scott Francis
Designed by Claudean Wheeler
Cover illustration by aaaniram / iStockphoto
Production coordinated by Debbie Thomas

About the Author

PHOTO © NYLA ALISIA

Sage Cohen is the author of *Writing the Life Poetic: An Invitation to Read and Write Poetry* and the poetry collection *Like the Heart, the World*. Her essay "The Word Is the Way" appeared alongside thought leaders such as Barack Obama, Al Gore, and Thomas L. Friedman in the anthology *How to Achieve a Heaven on Earth*. Sage has won first prize in the Ghost Road Press poetry contest and been nominated for a Pushcart Prize. She holds an M.A. in creative writing from New York University and a B.A. from Brown University. Sage lectures and teaches widely—including the popular online class Poetry for the People, publishes the Writing the Life Poetic zine, and has recently launched the online community and learning laboratory The Path of Possibility in Writing and Life at www.pathof possibility.com. In Portland, Oregon, Sage lives with her husband, a muse menagerie of three cats and two dogs, and the cutest toddler ever to say "duck." Visit Sage at www.sagecohentheproductivewriter.com.

Table of Contents

Introduction

WELCOME TO YOUR PRODUCTIVE WRITING LIFE

I AM A POET AND A BUSINESS WRITER, LEFT-HANDED AND right-footed. I write highly targeted, strategic marketing content by day, then get as loose and unstructured as I can by night to fumble about in the possibilities of poetry. I've spent the past twenty years cross-fertilizing strategies from both expressions of my life (and both sides of my brain) as a writing professional. Along the way, I have been filling in the middle ground with essays, articles, and nonfiction books.

What I've learned through this process is that productivity is a lifestyle choice. Just as a vegetarian reinforces daily this way of life with the food he chooses to eat, the Productive Writer holds a clear and meaningful value that gets expressed and explored in a myriad of ways every single day—in the writing she does, the relationships she has, the spirit in which she works, and the opportunities she creates to move toward her goals.

As nuanced and unique as our lives are, such is our relationship with productivity. Different types of writing have different demands, and every project and commitment will teach us something new about who we are, what we're made of, and what approaches bear repeating. This is the joy and the challenge of the writing life. We are never entering the same stream twice. And for many of us, the blank page will be intimidating no matter how many thousands of times we might face it.

Productivity, then, is your own, personal GPS as you navigate the endless wildernesses of your mind, craft, or subject matter and bring the best of what you have to offer to the page—and the world. Productivity is a means of witnessing and steering yourself toward your greatest good and training yourself to weed out the interference along the way.

The good news is that anything is possible in the realm of productivity if you are clear about the path or goal you are choosing, and committed to discovering and doing what it takes to get you there. Whether you are writing romance novels or technology white papers— or anything in between—if you'd like to express any part of your writing life more efficiently and effectively, with more joy and better results, this book is for you.

You will likely read some approaches throughout this book that sound promising and others that you wouldn't touch with a ten-foot lead. I invite you to experiment with the strategies and systems that appeal to you until you become your very own productivity expert, then fine-tune this system over time. Keep in mind that often it is the approach that seems least appealing or intuitive that offers the best results.

Are you ready to discover that what you want most in your writing life is not just possible but probable? Are you prepared to step into the rightful rhythms and productive practices that are yours and yours alone? Get ready to stake your claim on the writing life you most desire.

I hope this book proves good company as you vision, dream, and blueprint your own, personal productive writer possibilities—and then raise the barn with the systems, strategies, and attitudes that can transform you from A Person Who Writes into The Productive Writer. (No wardrobe change or phone booth required.)

To your success!

Chapter 1

EVERYONE HAS INSIDE HIM A PIECE OF GOOD news. The good news is that you don't realize how great you can be! How much you can love! What you can accomplish! And what your potential is!"

—ANNE FRANK, *author of* Anne Frank: The Diary of a Young Girl

JUST SAY YES

The phrase "Just Say No" is practically our national anthem. An endless array of empowerment and self-help books will advise you that putting this small-but-incisive word in your boundary arsenal is how you create the kind of structure and sanity you need in your life.

I would argue the opposite: You need a life that flows from YES. Before you can start making decisions about what you *don't* want, you would be well served to understand what you *do* want. If you have the big picture of YES mapped out clearly—and are grounded in your own passion and purpose—then it will be far easier to identify what's not a fit for you.

This chapter is your chance to decide what you are saying *yes* to in your writing life, so you can start turning your sails into that wind.

(And in chapter twelve, you'll learn about saying *no* to everything else.) Let's get to it, shall we?

PUTTING THE "YOU" IN PRODUCTIVITY

There is no other writer in the world who is trying to accomplish exactly what you are striving for, in the context of your unique personality, skills, education, training, work, family, and lifestyle mix. I invite you to define productivity in a way that is going to be specific and meaningful to you by considering both the personal and the universal.

On page 11 in this chapter, you'll find a questionnaire to guide you in articulating exactly what productivity means in your writing life, so you'll have your very own map to guide your very own journey. I also believe that there is a universal law of productivity that can help any writer navigate the endless choices we make about how we spend our time, and what we produce (and sell or publish). I call this law *The 3 Ps of Productivity*.

The 3 Ps of Productivity

1. PLEASURE	If you enjoy what you are doing, you'll be far more likely to continue doing it and eventually be successful at it.
2. POSSIBILITY	If you are clear about the value of any process, project, or opportunity—in other words, how it makes your goals, desires, and dreams more possible—you are far more likely to stay on course, even when the going gets rough.
3. PROSPERITY	Productivity does not deplete the stores. It fills you up—with confidence, expertise, money, information, inspiration, recognition, authority—maybe not all of these, all at once, but certainly in at least one or two key ways that register as "prosperous" for you.

When presented with an opportunity or evaluating a project that is in-process, consider how it measures up against these 3 Ps and decide from there whether it's the right fit for you.

MAKE A CASE FOR YOUR FUTURE

What if you don't know exactly what you want your writing life to be? No problem. Just as a lawyer builds a case for the argument she is making in court, imagine that you are making a case for your delighted and accomplished future as a person of letters. To this end, collect as evidence everything that might serve as a marker on your path, stretching your sense of the possible.

I recommend that you keep a separate file for each of the following categories that pertain to your writing and publishing goals. Every day, be on the lookout for inspiring examples that may inform or inspire a step you see yourself taking along your productive writing journey.

- **PUBLISHING POSSIBILITIES:** The names of presses, magazines, journals, or publishers whose published work feels familial with yours.

- **INSPIRING SAMPLES:** Pieces of writing that you admire.

- **KINDREDS:** Names of writers (and examples of their writing) whose work feels in some way related to yours.

- **LESSONS LEARNED:** How-to articles about topics you are learning, success (and failure) stories of writers in your field and not in your field; wisdom from thought leaders you admire.

- **BOOKS TO READ:** Reviews, recommendations from friends, and blog posts about books you intend to read. Including a few notes about why you've chosen each book can help you keep track of your list and what it means to you.

- **THINGS TO TRY:** Lessons to learn; classes to take; experiments to try with craft, form, or process—wherever YES takes you.

- **PEOPLE TO KNOW:** Potential agents, editors, collaborators, interview sources, mentors, teachers, colleagues. When reading writers

you admire, for example, write down names from the acknowledgments section, then go learn about those editors and agents. Or if you read an interview with an industry expert and get an idea for how you might approach that person, or someone in a similar role, in the future, make a note of it.

- **PLACES TO APPEAR:** Radio, newspapers, magazines and blogs that feature writers you enjoy, and where you would like to appear.

- **TEACHING:** Lectures, conferences, and other literary or professional gatherings that you can imagine yourself participating in as a speaker, teacher, or leader—either now or in the future.

- **READING:** Ongoing or one-time events in your community, or beyond, where you might like to read from your work.

- **POTENTIAL PARTNERS:** Businesses and people you'd like to explore collaborating with.

- **POTENTIAL CLIENTS TO APPROACH:** Businesses and people you believe could benefit from your writing or related products and services.

- **[YOUR OWN TOPICS HERE]**

The idea here is that by the time you're ready to publish or take a workshop or teach, you'll have a collection of great ideas that you've collected along the way to serve as reference points. This way, your future won't look like a great, white, empty page, but rather an overflowing collection of places and possibilities you've already navigated and can easily step into, without missing a beat.

STUDY YOUR HEROES

What writers do you admire most? How have they shaped their writing careers? With social media being what it is today, you can simply visit the websites or subscribe to the blogs of a few writers or authors you admire to start learning about how productivity looks in their lives, and how it is powering their success. A few things to observe are:

- How and when (and at what age) did this writer start publishing?
- What kinds of writing has he published, and in what order?
- What type of recognition has she received?
- What other, related types of work does this writer do, such as teaching, public speaking, writing in a day job?
- How does he present himself online, and what kind of relationship with readers is he developing?
- How many different types/genres of writing is this writer known for?
- What kind of life does she seem to live?
- What elements of this writer's big picture would I like to emulate in my own writing life?

You can cull your favorite strategies, techniques, and goals from this list; then put them to work for you. Another valuable reason to study as many writers as possible is to see how varied and unique the trajectory of every writing life is.

It can be tempting to fixate on some person we know, decide we can't do *it* (whatever "it" may be) the way they've done *it*, and give up. But when we see that there are endless ways to establish and sustain a productive writing life—at any age, in any work-family-life circumstance—we may have an easier time trusting that we will find our own way forward. Did you know that the poet Virginia Hamilton Adair, for example, published her first book of poetry at the age of eighty-three, to huge critical acclaim? Anything is possible in the writing life. Why not choose as your examples writers who remind you of this? Not so you can strive to do what they did, necessarily, but so you can get inspired to claim what is most authentic in your own life, no matter what the odds appear to be.

BUILD YOUR "PRODUCTIVE WRITER" BLUEPRINT

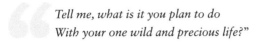

> *Tell me, what is it you plan to do*
> *With your one wild and precious life?"*
>
> —MARY OLIVER, *Pulitzer Prize–winning poet*

Dave Ellis, founder of Falling Awake and author of *Becoming A Master Student*, suggests that since we generally accomplish 25 percent of the goals we set, we should aim for Paradise × 4 in order to ultimately arrive at Paradise. I have found this to be one of the simplest and most effective strategies in my writing life. It gives me permission to dream bigger than what seems realistic. As a result, my experience of reality has expanded significantly as I've achieved the majority of my Paradise × 4 goals. As such, I have come to believe that the inverse of "That which we resist, persists," is "That which we name, we claim." Try it, I think you'll like it.

Aim High. Expect Low.

In the worksheet below, I've proposed a few categories for exploring the possibilities of your writing life and asked a question or two for each to help you start painting your own Paradise × 4 picture. Remember to aim wildly, embarrassingly high. And keep in mind that you're not expecting to get all the way to Paradise × 4—just to hold it in your sights as you appreciate where you are today and tomorrow. In other words, don't let your ideas of what's possible stop you from writing down your Big Dreams here.

My Paradise x 4 Writing Life

DIMENSION OF WRITING LIFE	PARADISE × 4 PROMPTS
GESTALT	What do you intend for your experience to be each time you sit down to write? (Inspired? Energized? Meditative?)
TIME	How many hours do you intend to write every week? What would the ideal pattern/rhythm be?
RESULTS	What are you striving to accomplish? • How much work do you want to produce each day/week/month? • How will you know when a piece is finished? • What are your intentions for finished work? (Do you want to publish it? Share it with friends? File it away?) • What steps will you take to fulfill those intentions?
SUCCESS	How do you define success, in any or all of the following: • Publication—how many times/which pieces per year? • Money—how much per month/year/decade do you intend to earn? • Awards—what awards or contests would you like to win? • Leadership opportunities—what/how many teaching or speaking gigs are you striving for this year? • Freedom/flexibility/continued time to write?
LIFESTYLE	What do you want your writing life to look like/feel like?
WRITING COMMUNITY	What kind of writing community do you intend to create? (See chapter sixteen to get a sense of what is possible.)
WORK/LIFE BALANCE	What is the ideal mix of time spent working (at a job)/sleeping/playing/with friends and family/writing? (On page 10 of this chapter, you'll be invited to create a pie chart so this picture becomes palpable for you.)

Keep in mind that your picture of Paradise × 4 will be continuously evolving. As you read this book, for example, you may have new ideas about what to expect from your writing life. Let your list be fluid as

you clarify your vision and hone your aspirations along the way. (In chapters four and seven, we'll transform your Big Dreams into achievable goals by breaking them down into scheduled, achievable tasks.)

Have Your Pie (and Slice It, Too)

If each day of your life were a pie, how would you divide it to deliver bigger slices of what you want most, and a balanced portion of the rest? Make a picture of what you'd like your daily pie to look like, and then refer to it often as you blend the raw ingredients of your life. I've included one very basic example of someone who is intending to write, work at a job, and spend time with his family. Your pie will include all of the slices that are meaningful to you—volunteering, spiritual life, exercise, reading, time with friends. And you may want to divide your "writing" slice into subsections of promoting, submitting, research, and any other relevant slivers that add up to the full slice. Let this image inspire you, but don't let it limit you. When it's time for a new picture, make one.

In chapter seven, you'll learn how to easily translate this picture to a schedule that reflects both your goals and your availability.

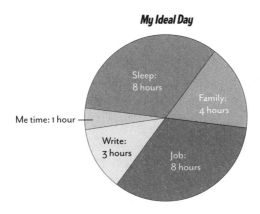

My Ideal Day

Choose a Word That Encapsulates Your Intentions

Having a single word as organizing principle for your Productive Writer aspirations can be very powerful. At the start of each year, I choose a word to define the big-picture goal I intend to strive for (and reach) in the coming year. In 2009, the year that my book *Writing the Life Poetic* was published, I chose the word *Author-ity* and posted it right over my desk. Everything I did that year in my writing life was organized around establishing and nurturing my relationship with this new archetype taking shape in me.

Think about what you want to feel, believe, accomplish, or become this year, and choose a word that is worthy of this goal. Then write it down somewhere visible, refer to it often, and let it remind you where you're headed.

LEARN WHAT PRODUCTIVITY MEANS TO YOU

Now that you've researched what is being accomplished in your field, made a case for your future, and dreamed big about your Productive Writing Life, let's drill down to some details of exactly who you are and what you want. Following are some questions you can consider as you start to articulate your personal productivity values and standards. I recommend that you write something down now, even if you're not sure of the answer, and return to these questions over time. It can be a useful record of how you are growing and what you are learning about yourself and your writing life.

Productivity Defined (by You!)

- How do I define "productive writing life"?
  - What does a productive writing life look and feel like? What does it accomplish? What are its "office hours" and

writing rhythms? What else, in addition to writing, happens in that life, and what is the work/life balance?
- What writers and authors do I admire?
- What can I learn from their unique or distinctive approaches to productivity?
- What have I read, observed, gleaned over the years about how a productive writing life gets established and nurtured?

- How am I productive today?
  - What am I accomplishing that I value?
  - What skills and strategies am I using to do so?
  - What technologies and tools are serving me best?
  - What attitudes and habits align with (will help me achieve) my values and goals?
  - Who in my community today is contributing to my productivity—through friendship, collaboration, mentorship, a critique group, writing dates, or something else?

- How do I intend to be more productive moving forward?
  - What do I want to accomplish in my writing life—both the big-picture long term, and the specifics of the immediate future?
  - What skills and strategies are likely to help me accomplish this?
  - What technologies and tools do I intend to learn and use, and how do I expect them to help me?
  - What habits or beliefs can I choose or improve to achieve greater productivity?
  - Is there additional knowledge or expertise that could help me become more productive?

- Who do I know (or who do I want to know), such as friends, colleagues, or teachers, who might help me become more productive?

ACT AS IF YOU ARE ALREADY THERE

Ready for a rather unconventional, yet surprisingly effective exercise? Write a letter to The Universe that gives thanks for every single detail of your imagined, future writing life—as if you are already there, experiencing all of the rewards. Scan your *Paradise × 4* list, flip through your *Making a Case* files, and imagine yourself to be inhabiting that wildly productive future you have dreamed up. From that place of prosperity, productivity, and pleasure, tell The Universe exactly how grateful you are for the accomplishment(s) you've manifested. Bring in all of your best craft skills to make this letter as palpable and vivid as you can. The more you can solidly place yourself into this imagined future and write AS IF you were already there, with humility and gratitude, the more likely you are to rewire yourself for this probability.

START RIGHT NOW

A tomato plant does not spontaneously appear out of the ground bearing ripe fruit. Nor does a writing life transform itself in an instant. You are cultivating the ground of a fertile and multifaceted life, and inviting it to bear a very specific type of fruit. Over time, with your kind attention, The Productive Writer will take root in you and blossom. Or maybe your productivity is already blossoming and simply needs a little pruning and fresh compost. Whether you are fine-tuning or taking your first step, start now. Turn the page. Write down an intention. Do what is yours to do, and the rest will follow.

Chapter 2

CLAIMING YOUR NORTH STAR: PLATFORM

THE WORD PLATFORM *SIMPLY DESCRIBES ALL THE ways you are visible and appealing to your future, potential, or actual readership."*

—CHRISTINA KATZ, *from* Get Known Before the Book Deal: Use Your Personal Strengths to Grow an Author Platform

The Productive Writer names and claims a platform and navigates by its light, because she understands:

- Platform is relevant to any writer, no matter what your topic, audience, or type of writing.
- Platform is your North Star; it helps you keep your eyes on the prize of whatever goal(s) you are striving to accomplish; it gives a clear context for those goals.
- Fueled by Productive Writer skills and strategies, your platform will likely grow—expanding your reach, reputation, and revenue.

Platform is the turf you claim and name as your area of expertise in your writing life, and it's everything you do to make that expertise visible. Just as a thesis is the foundation of a term paper around which its argument is built, a platform is an organizing principle around which a writer's many expressions of work revolve. A platform says to both the writer and the world, "I am an expert in [fill in the blank with your specialty]!" Yours should be a topic or craft or theme or audience that has energy and curiosity for you: one that you know about now and want to invest a whole lot more time knowing a whole lot more about.

With such clarity of purpose, over time you will likely publish, teach, lead, and share wisdom in ways that express, explore, and give shape to your expertise. And as this happens, you will start to become recognized as an authority in your chosen realm.

Platform is both the destination and the path. You build it as you go. It keeps you moving forward, tells you where forward is, and is the measure against which you decide if you're getting there.

I consider Christina Katz's *Get Known Before the Book Deal* to be the bible on this topic, offering everything a Productive Writer needs to know about establishing and developing her own platform. In this chapter, we'll cover the relationship between platform and productivity.

HOW A PLATFORM CAN HELP BOOST PRODUCTIVITY

- **FOCUS.** When you're clear about your topic or area of expertise, you know which writing, speaking, teaching, lecturing, and advising opportunities are a fit and which are not. This helps you grow your writing and career with clarity and intention.

- **MOMENTUM.** The more we write about our specialty, the more proficient we become. A rhythm is likely to start taking shape, and with it a momentum of confidence and accomplishment.

- **LEVERAGING SUCCESS.** Let's say you've written two or six or twenty articles about marketing for entrepreneurs. The more you write and publish, the greater your wealth of material to

draw from, repurpose, and repackage to new audiences. For example, you could adapt content published in a national business journal to a presentation for a local community of mom-owned businesses.

- **RELATIONSHIPS.** If you are clear that your expertise is writing technical manuals for computers or ghostwriting biographies for rock stars, this helps you choose and build meaningful relationships with the appropriate clients, colleagues, partners, agents, editors, networking and business development associations, and colleagues. If you know only that you're a "writer," where in the world do you begin to connect with the people in your field?

- **PUBLISHING.** Each type of writing has its own unique publishing market with a specific set of standards, rules, and key players. The more familiar you are with the rules of the road of any given market, the greater your odds of success. Knowing that you are focused on growing your poetry platform, for example, means that you can really focus on understanding which journals you admire and strive to publish in, and which publishers may be the right fit for your poems or manuscript.

- **AUTHORITY.** The more experience you have writing and publishing on your chosen platform specialty, the more you and the people in your field will trust in your authority.

- **OPPORTUNITY.** With visible authority comes opportunity. Once your dedication to your platform has earned you a reputable name in your given field, requests for your expertise—in the form of interviews, articles, speaking engagements, teaching, and more—may start rolling in. But more importantly, you will have paved the way to go after exactly what you want to create in your writing life, buoyed by the confidence that comes from proven experience.

WHY YOU NEED A PLATFORM

Poet, Fiction Writer, Essayist

- Continuously hone your craft, skill, and finished work.
- Build name recognition.
- Better understand your market and its unique opportunities.
- Increase your chances of publishing (both individual pieces and books).
- Improve the odds of winning prizes and receiving grants and residencies.
- Expand teaching, speaking, community leadership, mentoring, and other leadership opportunities.

Freelance Magazine Writer

Much of the above, plus:

- Become more targeted and effective in querying assignments.
- Increase your odds of landing the assignments you want.
- Establish yourself as a proven expert in your field/topic.
- Expand your reach to higher-profile, higher-paying work.
- Leverage your time, energy, and knowledge to most efficiently establish a growing body of work.
- Grow your platform into a nonfiction book, series of books, national speaking tour, or whatever you define as your long-term goal(s).

Business Writer

Much of the above, plus:

- Understand your field, your competition, your clients, and your prospects.
- Become more targeted and effective in attracting prospects and closing the deal.

- Know how to create bids that reflect what you're worth and the time you'll spend.
- Write content that meets client objectives, time frames, and budgets.
- Participate in the right business-building opportunities.
- Cultivate your network of prospects and clients.
- Earn more and more money in your day job so you have more time and freedom for your other writing platform(s).

Nonfiction Author

If you want to author a nonfiction book, a proven platform is the keystone to this edifice. Platform is the foundation upon which a successful proposal will be written, and the right agent and publisher will be acquired. Why? Because it proves that you've already established the two things that your book will demand: expertise on your topic and a community of interested readers.

THINK YOU DON'T HAVE A PLATFORM? THINK AGAIN!

Years ago, in a class taught by Christina Katz, students were asked to name and claim a platform. At that time, I had an advanced degree in poetry, dozens of publications, and various awards and residencies under my belt. I was hosting a monthly poetry reading series and read poems in the bathtub every night.

I had no idea what to choose for my platform. The list of topics I proposed ranged from "preparing for single motherhood" to "living with dogs."

Christina's gracious response was something to the effect of, *Seems to me that you are a poet.*

With this single sentence, a light bulb came on and then an entire stadium lit up inside of me.

In retrospect, it seems more than a little silly that I didn't see "being a poet" as an established platform. At that time, it didn't occur to me that poetry was platform worthy. Poetry was poetry, and I loved it and I read it and I wrote it—but what was I going to say to the world about it?

That week, I named my platform "Writing the Life Poetic." And within a year, I was negotiating a book deal by that same name.

Don't think you have a platform? I'll bet it's right under your latte, and you don't even know it.

What type of writing are you doing right now? What topic have you been madly in love with for as long as you can remember? What does everyone at work come to you to solve when they can't do it themselves? What did your high school yearbook say about you? What does your mother brag about to her friends when your name comes up? Take a step back from what you think a platform is supposed to be and do, and simply think about who you are. This is where you will find your platform. It is woven into the fabric of your life, so integrated with who you are that it barely calls attention to itself. If you parse out the threads of the weave, I'll bet you your first paycheck that it will be there.

I'll show you mine if you show me yours!

Your Platform at a Glance

PLATFORM BUILDING BLOCKS	INSIGHTS
Theme, topic, genre, or area of expertise	Poetry for the people, with a goal of encouraging writers of all levels to write, read, and enjoy poetry.
Audience(s) you serve	• People who feel afraid, unwelcome, or unsure of how to start writing poetry. • People already writing poetry who want to write more, improve their craft, and have more fun. • Writers of all stripes wanting to invigorate their relationship with language.

Value you bring to each different type of reader	• People who feel afraid: Friendly encouragement and useful information.
	• People already writing poetry: Vast selection of tips, tools, strategies, and examples.
	• Writers of all stripes: A way into—and an enjoyable exploration of—the life poetic.
	• People who feel afraid: Want to be invited in to poetry and assured that they are welcome/can do it.
	• People already writing poetry: Seeking tools, techniques, and tips to help improve their craft.
	• Writers of all stripes: Seeking a poetic lens through which to better appreciate and apply language in anything and everything they write.
Platform name	Writing the Life Poetic
Why you are the ideal person to develop this platform over time	I have more than twenty years of experience cultivating a poetic way of life. I have an advanced degree in creative writing, a great deal of teaching experience, and a well-established career of writing and publishing poetry.
Why you are passionate about doing so	Poetry matters—not just as a literary form, but as a way of life. I know from my own experience that a relationship with poetry can significantly expand a person's sense of possibility, delight, and camaraderie with one's own being, universal human truths, and life itself. I want to make this gift available to anyone who's interested in receiving it.

 Create your own Platform-at-a-Glance worksheet.
Download available at writersdigest.com/article/productive-writer-downloads.

PUBLISHING VS. PLATFORM

Which came first, the publishing or the platform? This seems to be a topic of some confusion for folks. So let's break it down.

Platform is about becoming a recognizable expert. The book publishing ideal is to first build a platform, and then leverage that platform to pitch, sell, and write the book. But there are many stages of publishing (articles, essays, poems, stories) along the way that precede becoming an author and contribute to growing a platform. And for many writers, those early stages of publishing can be slow going.

The good news is that there are many ways to grow your visibility as an expert in your field that are available to you right now. So while you're waiting, for example, for your next short story to find a safe landing in just the right literary journal, there is much you could be doing to develop your platform, including:

- Teach what you know.
- Self-publish: Write and sell instructional e-books or publish print-on-demand collections of your creative writing (only if you are not seeking "mainstream" publication for this work).
- Join a literary collective and create (and publish) in community.
- Offer tips, insights, articles, and links via a blog, Twitter, Facebook, or Squidoo.
- Read your work publicly as much as possible.
- Become active in an online community that deals with your topic.
- Start your own online community to explore your topic.
- Offer coaching, consulting, or editing in your field.
- Create a subscription publication, such as an e-zine or newsletter.
- Join organizations in your field that allow you to gather and share ideas and opportunities with like-minded others.
- Publish magazine or newspaper articles on your topic or expertise.
- Share content with businesses or organizations that serve people in your area of expertise. (For example, if your platform is dog training, maybe local pet stores would want to feature a Q&A with you on their websites or as part of their monthly newsletters.)

POLYAMOROUS PLATFORMS: JUGGLING PUPPIES

> *When I'm writing for creativity and business, I always feel like I'm juggling about a million plates. Actually, it's more like two plates, two balls, a flaming stick, four chainsaws and a puppy. I don't want to drop any of them and I want to wow my audience, all without killing myself in the process."*
>
> —Shanna Germain, *award-winning poet, fiction writer, and freelance writer*

It is Valentine's Day, and I just read an interview where a polyamorous couple explained how they negotiate their primary relationship alongside various satellite love affairs. As I was contemplating how a couple might pull off the nitty-gritty logistics of such a lifestyle, it occurred to me that having two or more relationships may be like having two or more platforms—requiring multiple Valentine's Day celebrations, some very sophisticated calendaring, and an uncanny competence for, well, juggling flames and chainsaws and puppies.

What to do when one lover wants to sit under the covers and work through last night's conflict when you already have a date to go horseback riding with another? How to give direction and priority to two important, and sometimes-at-odds, platform trajectories galloping through your writing life?

Some writers simply need to have multiple irons in various platform fires or they're bored, stifled, stuck, enervated. Others who perceive multiple platforms to be a chaos of distraction choose a single topic then excavate every facet of it for every possible audience and market for the rest of their writing days.

There is a third, middle way that unifies a writer's various, unrelated platforms within an umbrella context. For example, my first platform was "Writing the Life Poetic." My second platform is now "The Productive Writer." (Each platform name happens to pair with a book title, but this is not the rule, it's just how it worked out for me.)

Keeping two different platforms chugging along independent of each other, on top of everything else I'm already doing, seems like more fish to fry than I have pans. So I'm in the process of establishing a bigger, more inclusive platform, which I'm calling "The Path of Possibility in Writing and Life." Within this umbrella, all of the writing topics I currently know, teach, and publish about are covered: productivity, poetry, creative nonfiction, authoring, motherhood, marketing writing, and promotion. It also gives me room to expand in directions I may not have yet imagined.

If we are to return to the polyamory metaphor, this kind of platform, then, becomes something akin to a multiple-partner marriage; one in which there is an agreed-upon family system within which various lives and loves turn—interdependently, and with a shared context and commitment. "Writing Your Life" is my new North Star—one I refer to every day to help me steer this burgeoning craft of my writing life in an integrated way that makes sense to me—and hopefully, will help me make sense to my readers.

How do your temperament and work style align with these possibilities? Are you most likely to be a platform monogamist or puppy juggler? Writer, writer, Productive Writer, how does your platform grow?

To Go Incognito or Integrate: That Is the Question

So you're a business writer and romance novelist. Or you have authored multiple nonfiction books on different topics. Or you want to develop your expertise on dog training in tandem with your syndicated relationship advice column. Shanna Germain writes about sex, coffee, death, and better living. She has chosen a single portal (a

unified website) to represent them all. What are you going to do with your mishmash of platforms and identities? Do you want a pen name for each platform? Are you willing to showcase your erotica publications through a presence well traveled by your corporate bank customers? These are personal integrity and strategic business decisions that only you can make.

I have chosen to keep my business writing and creative writing platforms entirely separate because I don't perceive any advantage in informing one audience about the other. My business clients don't care about Pushcart Prizes, and my literary community doesn't give a whit that I can write a kick-ass brochure. Why bore them with having to wade through information that is irrelevant? And why distract them from what I really want to be known about each particular realm of expertise?

So, I present myself like this. Each community connects with me through a different website and e-mail address. I use Sagecohen.com for my day job as a copywriter and Sagesaidso.com to represent my literary life. The language, imagery, and content of each site are completely different. The information I share about who I am and what I do are different. Each is written in a voice that reflects the platform it is representing.

I have colleagues who have such completely distinct platforms, complete with unique pen names, that they will not be photographed, lest they risk divulging their true identity. And there are others—you've heard from Shanna Germain—who say *This is the big, heaping plate full of who I am and what I write—take it or leave it.* You'll have to decide the best way to serve yourself, your family, the people you work for, and the people you write for in deciding whether to go incognito or integrate.

COHERENCE AND YOUR WRITING SOUL

These days, readers expect to have a personal connection with the writers they enjoy through their websites, blogs, teaching, and live appearances. Plus, with the widespread use of social media bridging the space between writer and reader, anyone who has admired your work can tap into your moment-by-moment publicized thinking through communities like Facebook and Twitter.

Therefore, who you are (or more accurately, how you present yourself publicly) and what you write are often one continuous experience for readers. This means that everything down to the shoes you choose when you give a reading can contribute to—or detract from—the evolution of your platform. For example, if you write cheery, uplifting self-help books, don't be a jerk to the clerk in the checkout line—any checkout line—ever.

I'm not saying that you shouldn't be who you are, or that you should be faking a personality to match your platform. But I am saying that you should be aware of how your life, your public image, and your writing resonate with each other, because the people listening to you will be aware of it. In my experience, coherence of these three elements makes for the smoothest and most streamlined ride for everyone involved—especially you. A writing life that grows out of who you authentically are is going to be the most grounded and sustainable path to success.

My friend Dan Raphael is an example of someone who has built a writing empire on the foundation of his wildly entertaining and unusual command of language and life. On the back of one of Dan's books is a quote that says:

> **SHE:** Do you think he's ever taken acid?
> **HE:** Taken it? I think he wears a patch.

Dan delivers on this very engaging and entertaining promise. He is a transcendent force of nature and engaging linguistic acrobatics on stage when delivering his poems and behind the scenes, when sending e-mail to friends.

If you have multiple writing platforms, it is important to consider what the expression of each one is in your life, and to be thoughtful about how you hold these layers of identity as your expertise grows and you become more visible.

I have another friend who is a widely sought photographer who has recently been recognized in several national magazines. This photographer has a parallel platform as a poet, and a good number of her poems explore the socioeconomic dynamics of being a person providing a service for the elite and the wealthy. This presents a bit of a platform pretzel, as she has no desire to alienate valued clients with her poetry. The expert photographer/poet is very delicately navigating how to hold these two parts of her life with integrity and authenticity as she quickly becomes more visible and respected in both chosen fields.

How is your life in alignment or out of whack with your platform(s) today? Is there anything you need to reconcile to create a greater coherence between what you write and how you live? How will you hold multiple platforms that represent different facets of who you are? Is there a way to unify them? Do you want to?

Chapter 3

THINKING PRODUCTIVE THOUGHTS

> *A PROFESSIONAL WRITER IS AN AMATEUR WHO didn't quit."*
>
> —RICHARD BACH, *author of* Jonathan Livingston Seagull

Being productive is not just about what you do; it is also about what you think and believe. In fact, our attitudes and the stories we tell ourselves might be the key to maximizing productivity in our writing lives.

Let's explore some Jedi mind-control maneuvers to keep your eyes on the prize, your butt in the chair, and your pen on the page.

YOU HAVE EVERYTHING YOU NEED TO WRITE RIGHT NOW

Instead of reading this chapter, you could be writing. You have choices; you make them all day long, often without noticing that the habits and rhythms you have are actually composed of a series of decisions that you made at one time and continue to make every time you repeat them. If you are in the habit of thinking that you don't have [fill in the blank with your loudest protest here] that you need to write, it's time to start thinking some new thoughts. Try this one: *I have a pen and a piece of paper. I have hands that work and eyes that see. I have thoughts and feelings and insights and images, and I can write them down. Once I even had an English teacher who insisted that I learn a*

little grammar. Everything I need to write is right here, right now. All I need to do is say Yes and go.

Don't idealize your way out of a writing life: You have everything you need to write this minute. What are you waiting for?

FROM DISCIPLINE TO DESIRE

Discipline gets the job done. But if you are not fueling it with the right energy source, it could become an inflexible, joyless rod that you come to dread rather than anticipate. Who wants to write just because we've told ourselves we have to? I want more from my writing life than that, and I want more for your writing life, too.

Discipline keeps us moving toward our goals. It keeps our minds churning and our hands moving across the keyboard or page with our imagined end in sight. May I be so bold as to suggest that you fuel this important practice with the nectar of the gods: desire?

Desire brings in the body, the soul, the spirit, and embraces the messy wonder of who we are. With desire as fuel, I propose that we delight in the process of writing; delight in the imagined state of completion; delight in the mind-jumbling confusion of not understanding how to get there; delight when the client or editor says, "Start over again, the voice isn't quite right and it's due in an hour"; delight in watching drafts unfurl like petals of something growing and dying and replenishing itself again; delight in checking tasks and days off the calendar, in depositing checks, in knowing that in this very moment, we are doing what we were put on this Earth to do—to write.

YOU ONLY NEED TO SEE WHAT'S IN FRONT OF YOU

In the movie *The Secret*, Jack Canfield talks about how easy it is to get tripped up by big-picture goals because they seem so daunting we can't imagine how we'll get there. In answer to this challenge, he explains that he drove in the dark all the way from California to New York, seeing with his headlights only two hundred feet ahead of him at a time.

I find this to be a reassuring metaphor for the writing life. We can only be responsible for two things: deciding where we're headed and moving as far as we can see right now in that direction. We don't have to understand the entire journey. But when we're clear about our destination and take small consistent steps in that direction, we may be surprised to find ourselves clear across the country in no time at all.

DO YOUR BEST, THEN LET GO

IN YOUR CONTROL	OUT OF YOUR HANDS
A commitment to defining and developing a platform.	The size and composition of the audience attracted to your work and platform.
A commitment to your craft .	The ultimate outcome of the work you produce. (You can only do your best.)
Research and understanding of your market.	Subjectivity, business priorities, and editorial decisions of editors.
A regular practice of sending work out for publication.	Who chooses to publish your work—and when.
Your attitude.	The judgments and perceptions of others.
Your care of your mind, body, and spirit.	Surprises, obstacles, and rewards along the way.
Your auxiliary commitments and responsibilities that limit or enhance writing opportunities.	Necessary work to care for your family or your home, or to do what is required at your job.
Your sleep.	May the sleep muse meet you there!
Your partner, children, and/or pets (the choices and promises you make).	Your partner, children, and/or pets (the choices they make, and the consequences for you).

DON'T WORRY; BE HAPPY

Writers are up against a lot when it comes to keeping our practice vital, engaged, and productive. We don't have time. We don't have energy. Blah, blah, blah. What if we were to turn our attention to what is actually working well, what is giving us energy, and what is seeming possible in this moment—no matter how small it might be?

In my experience, when we are truly dedicated to what is positive and possible, much of the negative stuff we've been feeding with our time and attention simply untangles itself in the background—just as any living thing given attention thrives, and any that is not tended eventually starves. Tend your satisfaction, and it will take root and flourish. This is fertile ground for your writing, your publishing, and your life.

SEND PROBLEMS PACKING

Years ago, my friend Mariko offered a simple thought-management trick when I was struggling with a personal problem that was affecting my ability to concentrate at work. On a small sticky note, she drew a little suitcase and stuck it to my computer screen. "Put your troubles in here," she said, "and imagine them on a revolving luggage rack above your head. They will be there when you're ready for them; but for now, you can take care of other stuff."

So that's exactly what I did: I visualized packing up my distracting thoughts into that suitcase and sent it revolving in the ether. It was surprisingly comforting to realize that I didn't have to give up the problem I was facing, I just had to find somewhere specific to put it so that I could carry on with everything else that needed doing. This device served me so well that there's a sticky note with a little suitcase on my computer screen right now. This suitcase has a happy face, reminding me that I can continue to invest in the negative story line I'm worrying like a religious practice, or I can choose to write this chapter.

UNTANGLING THE KNOT

When you're really stuck with your writing, you've tried everything and nothing is working, back off. Think of the knot which, when yanked, becomes only tighter. The trick is to loosen things up. Pretend you're busy doing something else. Put it in a drawer. Trust time. When you are preparing for bed, invite your sleeping self to find a solution. Then let it go. When you are out hiking, invite the sky to find a solution. Then let it go. When you call in an answer from the mystery where answers live, you can relax a little into the not knowing. Think of yourself as a child learning how to stand still so the frightened bird can trust your arm as a safe landing. You are training yourself to a new kind of answer. One that is already there, and you are learning how to listen.

KEEP YOUR INNER EDITOR TOO BUSY TO INTERFERE

There will be plenty of work for your inner editor to do when the time comes. But until it is time, a great way to keep interference to a minimum is to keep that naysayer busy doing something important.

For example, when I'm doing freewriting, one of my favorite writing calisthenics for getting loose and ready for action, I'll put my editor in charge of counting pages, keeping time, insisting that my hand keep moving, and demanding that I turn away from deliberate, thinking-triggered writing. Basically, my editor facilitates the mechanics of the process so my mind is free to wander. With such an important job to do, my editor is far too busy to start throwing her weight around; she knows she'll have ample time to judge the nonsense I'm scribbling later. For now, she gets to be the taskmaster supervising the scribble.

How can you occupy your own, well-meaning inner editor (who wants so badly for you to be successful that she's willing to say any mean thing to get you there) with some useful but tangential job—so you can have the space you need to create free of judgment?

COMPETITION KILLS

A universal truth in the writing life is that the moment we allow ourselves even the teeniest hierarchal thought, something tender in us clamps down and says "not possible."

Let's face it: Hierarchy is the psychological masonry of many cultures today. And the nature of the publishing business is to draw a line, subjective as it may be, between "worthy of publishing" and "not worthy of publishing." Plus, there are teachers and authors and writers everywhere who are resting their own fragile and insecure laurels on whatever rung in the ladder they're precariously perched on, who will look down on you and invite you to feel small.

What I'd like to remind you is that you have a choice. You can grasp that stone of "best, better, good, not good enough" and let it sink you. Or you can put it down beside you and keep writing. Only you can allow yourself to feel small next to someone you believe is bigger. And only you can choose to see in someone "higher up" than you the beacon of possibility for your own writing life. All you need to worry about (or, rather, enjoy) is your own good, better, and best, because that is what belongs to you. Do you see yourself making progress toward your goals? Can you appreciate your own tenacious spirit that simply stays focused on where you're headed? Don't distract yourself with feeling bad about what someone else is doing when there is so much to feel good about that is right in front of you.

PRODUCTIVE LICENSE GRANTED

Last year, I attended a workshop with Susan G. Wooldridge, author of *poemcrazy*. This extravagantly colorful, frenetic butterfly of a woman seemed to awaken each person in the room to his or her own stirring nectars. *This is possible! And this! And this!* was the subtext of everything Wooldridge offered and taught that afternoon. And at the end of the workshop, she passed around lovely, little business-sized cards that had a hand-drawn look to them. Each card said "Poetic License."

I love this idea of actually carrying a prop, a prompt, a permission to do and be the kind of writer we are striving to become. I think honoring our choices with some small symbol that says "I choose to be a Productive Writer" can actually make this path more possible.

BE GENTLE WITH YOURSELF

The only one who can make sure your writing life is a success is you. The only one who can define what success even means in your life is you. For one person, success is finding an early morning hour once a week to write absolution into that blank page. For another, success is publishing a twelve-book, best-selling adventure series featuring dragon toads that speak a language only tweens can understand.

Sometimes it can be tempting to view ourselves as hostage to our own goals or process. Please don't. Remember that you get to decide when it's time to work, sleep, eat peanut butter, and blow dandelion seeds into the wind. You get to set goals and timing—and change them if they're not serving you.

The liberating and sometimes terrifying truth is that you are entirely in charge here. The rules of the road are yours and yours alone. In your writing life, you are the CEO, CFO, the middle manager, the grunt worker, the secretary, bus driver, and janitor. Spoiler alert: You are not going to be good at everything at first, or ever. You are going to be as gawky and wobbly and strange and embarrassing as every being is when it's figuring out how to exist in a new context. This is how success looks in its early stages—like a mess. And then that mess starts taking shape.

Chapter 4

> *THERE IS NO SYSTEM, FORMULA, SOFTWARE, OR set of lists, no matter how completely filled out, that can tie together the almost infinite number of variables that go into 'getting our act together.' The only thing that makes it work is a consistent intervention of you. At some point you must lift yourself out of day-to-day tree-hugging and do at least a modicum of forest management."*
>
> —DAVID ALLEN, *author of* Getting Things Done and Getting More Out of Life

GET THE BIG PICTURE

In order to navigate in some comprehensible direction through space, we need a compass. And in order to navigate in some meaningful way through the jumble of to-dos on our list, we need a big-picture plan. So let's make one! This example reflects a writing life that includes a diverse spectrum of types of writing and goals.

My Writing Goals This Year

WRITING-LIFE CATEGORY	GOAL
Writing	· Complete my poetry collection.
	· Complete my nonfiction book proposal.
	· Complete one article query (and ideally the article) or personal essay per month.
	· Improve my craft, gain momentum, and get clearer about where I'm headed.
Submitting/pitching/ proposing	· Have three queries for magazine articles or personal essays in circulation at all times.
	· Submit poems to at least three publications or contests every month.
	· Distribute book proposal to agents.
	· Distribute poetry collection to publishers.
Platform development	· Publish at least six poems.
	· Write a monthly column that reflects my platform expertise for my local writing association's newspaper.
	· Sell three to six articles or essays to national magazines.
	· Teach five weekend workshops and four six-week classes in my area of expertise.
	· Read or lecture monthly.
Community building/ education/inspiration	· Attend at least two writers conferences.
	· Attend at least one literary event per month.
	· Host and promote a monthly reading series.

Piece of cake, right? Or as per our visioning in chapter one, it would be more accurate to say, *Piece of pie*! The question is, how do we fit all of this juicy filling into that single pie slice called "My Productive Writing Life"? Let's find out.

Slivering the Slice

In chapter one, we worked out a plan for a writer with a day job that afforded three hours of writing per day. Let's say that same writer created the annual writing goals above. Here are a few ways he might sliver the writing slice:

- 1 hour/day: write poetry
- 1 hour/day: write magazine articles or essays
- 1 hour/day: query/proposal/submissions work

Or like this:

- Mondays, 3 hours: write poetry
- Tuesdays, 3 hours: write magazine articles or essays
- Wednesdays, 3 hours: query/proposal/submissions work
- Thursdays, 3 hours: write poetry
- Fridays, 3 hours: write magazine articles or essays
- Saturdays, 3 hours: query/proposal/submissions work

Or maybe she'd break out a few of her hours each week for promotion/platform development. And a few for reading, learning, and generally filling her cup.

You get the gist. How you organize the slice depends on the rhythms that work best for you. And it may be different from day to day or week to week. What's important to remember is that when you know how much time you have and you have a big picture of what you want to accomplish in that time, it becomes far simpler to figure out what thread you might want to pick up when you sit down at your desk (or the bleachers at your kids' school, or wherever you are) to write. And as you develop a specific rhythm that you replicate with some regularity over time, you'll get faster and more efficient at getting in the groove and making things happen there. (In chapter seven,

you'll learn how to structure your work hours to reflect your goals using a variety of time-management tools.)

PAY YOURSELF FIRST

> *I write from the adage of 'pay yourself first.' This works for time as well as money. I never answer my phone before noon. My writing and work time runs from about 8:30 A.M. to noon each day. Once I'm done with my own work, I'm happy to talk to others, including family, students, clients, or colleagues."*

—GREGORY A. KOMPES, *author of* Suddenly Psychic: Core Messages to Enhance Your Psychic Journey

Financial experts recommend that you pay yourself first—putting money into emergency savings, IRA accounts, and other such investments in your future—before paying everyone else you owe. The most productive writers I know live by the same rule: They invest in themselves by spending time on writing as the first priority, no matter how many other priorities they have in their full and fabulous lives. If you were to commit to paying your Productive Writer self first, what would that look like for you?

Find New Ways to Pay Yourself First

We all have rhythms for working and living that have been going on for so long that they seem like our only options. This may or may not be true. The fact is, we all face a unique mix of freedoms and limitations when it comes to paying ourselves first. Want to find out if you have more wiggle room for writing than you imagined? Consider these questions:

- What entertainment activities could I go without, and write instead?
- Could I find extra time to write on my way to or home from work?

- Could I wake up a little earlier and write before my day starts?
- Could I ask my partner for help with the kids so I get a two-hour chunk of writing time on a weekday night or weekend afternoon?
- Am I willing to allow my butt to expand a bit as I trade every other gym visit for a writing session?
- Is there a neighborhood playgroup I could join with my small children to create one morning for myself every week?
- Could I afford to cut back my hours at work?
- Would a different type of work leave me with more energy or time for writing? (And would I be willing to change jobs or careers or income to accomplish this?)
- What, specifically, do I need in the way of writing time, and who can I ask for help?
- What have I done successfully in the past to create time and space to write?
- What am I doing in my life right now that is working for my writing goals?
- Am I giving time to someone or something else right now that I can reassign to writing?
- How could I make the writing I do for money create time and energy for the writing I do for love?
- How could I work more efficiently at home or work so I get results (and finish) faster?
- Can I afford a babysitter or a writing retreat?
- What do I believe about not having enough of what I need to write? How can I rewrite that belief, starting today?

As you consider the questions on this list that pertain to your situation, you will get a sense of how much you value your writing life, how much you are willing to make space for it in the context of your many commitments, and exactly what you are ready and able to renegotiate to start investing in yourself.

BREAK IT DOWN AND PACE YOURSELF

I make my to-do list with the smallest common denominator. It's much less intimidating to approach a list with small, specific items than one big task. Instead of "write 2,000-word assigned article about real estate market," I will write:

1. "e-mail Realtor to schedule interview"

2. "find statistic on current average home value"

3. "call Association of Realtors to request they mail materials"

—WENDY BURT-THOMAS, *author of* The Writer's Digest Guide to Query Letters

Thanks to the work you've done in this chapter, you are clear about your big-picture goals, you have your designated hours per week to dedicate to them, and you're committed to squeezing every drop out of every minute you have. Now what?

Let's say you are offering a writing workshop (as listed under "platform development" on your annual goals list) two months from today, but you have never promoted an event before and will be starting at ground zero. One step at a time, one day at a time, you can establish a solid system for getting the word out. We'll do it together right here to give you a feel for the rhythm.

1. First, brainstorm a list of things you can do to let folks know about your event.
2. Second, set weekly targets for high-level goals.
3. Finally, break it into bite-size to-dos and plan to take one small step every day.

Promotional Brainstorm:

- Update e-mail signature to include event information.

- Send a press kit to targeted media list (details about key components on page 193).
- Write blog post inviting readers to attend.
- Send announcement to local e-lists and calendars for writers at least a week before.
- Make an announcement on Facebook.
- Tweet about it using Twitter.
- Send a message to targeted friends or groups on Facebook.
- Invite friends and colleagues directly by e-mail, with an opt-out option (so you'll know that anyone who doesn't wish to receive these invitations can easily get off of your list).
- Offer tips from your workshop to blogs that are related to yours, with a link to your event information.
- Offer free content reflecting your workshop topic to local writing organizations' newsletters.

Weekly and Daily Break-Down:

Week 1: Research and establish targeted media list and local e-lists

DAY	TASK	TIME
Day 1	Set up ConstantContact e-mail marketing account.	10 minutes
Day 2	Research and compile contact info for local literary e-lists and calendars.	5 minutes
Day 3	Research and compile contact info for appropriate media. (Timing depends on how deep you go with research; you can always spread this step over a number of days.)	15-60 minutes
Day 4	Create "media" e-mail list in ConstantContact and enter contact info from Day 2 and Day 3 research.	15 minutes
Day 5	Write one-paragraph blurb about the workshop that describes who it's for, three key results it will offer participants, location and time, and registration information.	15 minutes

Day 6	Add to blurb written on Day 5: a one-paragraph bio describing your expertise, publishing history, and other relevant info about your education or experience. Include three testimonials of satisfied students or previous workshop participants, if you have them.	15 minutes
Day 7	Post class and bio info on your blog with a headline that makes its value clear.	10 minutes
	Add short, inviting event teaser to e-mail signature line with a link to blog post. (For the next six weeks, every e-mail you send will become a promotion.)	
	Announce workshop on Facebook, with a link to blog post.	
	Tweet about the workshop; link to blog.	

Week 2: Write and send press release/media kit (four weeks before the event)

DAY	TASK	TIME
Day 1	Get tips for writing an effective press release and see a great example in Christina Katz's *Get Known Before the Book Deal.*	10 minutes
Day 2	Using your blog post as a starting place, compose a press release that highlights the unique value of this event, focusing on the results/benefits for participants, plus provides all key event and contact info, with a link to your online media page.	15-30 minutes
Day 3	Update media page on blog or website with links to, or downloads of, latest clips, interviews, etc.	15-30 minutes
Day 4	Create press release in ConstantContact and distribute to targeted list.	15 minutes
Day 5	Archive your press release in a system that is easy to use and reference. Enter key info in your log. (See page 68 for more details.)	15 minutes
Day 6	Jot down a list of ideas or intentions for expanding your media list the next time you are promoting a workshop.	10 minutes
Day 7	Go get a fancy coffee drink and pat yourself on the back for a job well done.	15 minutes

Week 3: Reach out directly to your community of writers

DAY	TASK	TIME
Day 1	Research and compile contact info for local writing organizations.	10 minutes
Day 2	Prepare a one-to-two paragraph tip lifted from your workshop. As part of your brief byline, add a single sentence about the name/date of your workshop with a link to registration info.	15-30 minutes
Day 3	Send the tip to contact list from Day 1; invite them to share tip with newsletter or e-mail list subscribers.	10 minutes
Day 4	Compile list of your favorite bloggers in your field.	15 minutes
Day 5	Send the tip to contact list from Day 4; invite them to share tip on their blogs. Post tip on your own blog with reminder about workshop details and registration.	15 minutes
Day 6	Compile a list of your friends and colleagues who might want to know about this event into a ConstantContact list. Send them an invite; to make it easy, copy and paste the information you wrote on your blog. (The advantage of using ConstantContact for this e-mail distribution is that recipients can always unsubscribe, so you don't have to worry about pestering them.)	15 minutes
Day 7	Announce tip on Facebook with link to blog. Tweet about the tip; link to blog.	5 minutes

Look at that—in just three weeks, for a few minutes each day, you've done all of the heavy lifting to promote your event—with three weeks to spare. In the coming weeks, you can continue to offer a new tip per week through your blog and Facebook, reinforced with a tweet or two, then send a reminder e-mail to your personal list a few days before the event, and you'll have covered all of your bases.

When you pace yourself day by day, week by week, you can accomplish quite a lot in small margins of time. And once you have foundational pieces of the puzzle in place—a press release template, bio, media list and personal contact list—promotion will get much faster. With three or four events under your belt, you'll have your own rhythm for making it happen. Before you know it, spreading the word will become second nature, and maybe even fun!

I recommend that you use the time log in chapter seven to help decide where you have fifteen minutes every day to dedicate to promotion. Then plug this task into your calendar so there's no question about making it happen.

TOP TEN PRODUCTIVITY BUSTERS

1. **NO BIG-PICTURE VISION.** If you don't have a vision for what you want and where you're headed in your writing life, it will be impossible to set realistic goals and measure your progress and productivity along the way. (Platform is a great way to focus your energies in a clear direction around which all of your writing work will revolve.)

2. **NO SHORT-TERM GOALS.** You can't hit a target that you can't see. Knowing your daily, weekly, monthly, and annual goals (both practical and aspirational) can help ensure that you keep moving in the right direction—and that you know when you've arrived.

3. **FEAR.** Risk is the hinge on which productivity turns; if we are not in danger of failing, we are not likely growing. When we let fear prevent us from taking steps that could bring our writing goals and dreams closer, we clamp down on our possibilities and limit our opportunities to succeed.

4. **DOING THE WRONG TASK AT THE WRONG TIME.** Understanding your own writing rhythms and honoring them is the key to finding and sustaining a flow that you can count on. For example, I have come to the unfortunate conclusion that I have ants in

my pants until about 4:00 P.M. The popular wisdom is that the early morning is "the time" for a writer. If I had limited myself to writing in this prescribed time that is not a fit with my biorhythm, surely I would have given up by now.

5. **SHABBY SYSTEMS.** If you can't find the latest draft of your essay, don't remember what you've pitched and to whom, can't keep track of the great ideas you're having, and have no system for archiving, measuring, repeating, and building on success, this is likely to limit your performance, satisfaction, and results.

6. **LACK OF CREATIVITY AND CONSCIOUSNESS ABOUT TIME.** If you're not aware of how you're spending time, what your time is worth, how you might source more writing hours from the life you're living right now, or what you intend to accomplish in each chunk of writing time you do have, you are not getting the best value from this most precious resource.

7. **TRANSITION TURBULENCE.** Without solid systems and established rhythms for sitting down to the blank page, completing a writing session, or generally navigating the unbounded freedoms of being responsible for our own motivation and performance, we are likely to have bumpy transitions that can limit our productivity and discourage us from even attempting to get started.

8. **PERFECTIONISM.** If you wait for your work to be perfect, it (and you) may never leave your desk. If you focus, instead, on professionalism—doing the very best that you can, committing to learn along the way, and understanding that mistakes and failures are the nurse logs that feed every success, you can steadily improve without that albatross of the impossible weighing you down.

9. **ISOLATION.** Writers need other people to learn with and from. We need a context in which to understand and appreciate the work that we are doing. We need role models whose accom-

plishments we can aspire to, colleagues we can conspire with, and business partners who can collaborate with us to bring our work forward. Without a social, professional, and community context, we are far more likely to get discouraged, lose our way, and miss out on opportunities for greater pleasure, prosperity, and productivity.

10. **NEGLECTING TO CELEBRATE AND BE GRATEFUL.** It's easy to focus on the negative in writing and in life; there is certainly plenty of opportunity to do so. But when we, instead, turn our attention to what's working and what we appreciate from moment to moment, something surprising happens—our sails turn into the wind. Let me be clear, I'm talking about the smallest of celebrations: for the blank sheet of paper drinking up the ink under your hand, the sun pointing a finger through the curtain to your desk, the editor who included a personal note in the form rejection letter.

Chapter 5

CAPTURING, SAVING, AND REPURPOSING IDEAS

THE PRODUCTIVE WRITER GENERATES IDEA EQUITY BY:

- Paying attention and practicing receptivity.
- Creating effective systems for capturing ideas.
- Storing ideas where they are easy to find and use.
- Saving every scrap of writing from the cutting floor.
- Using writing leftovers as inspiration or source material for new writing.
- Repurposing existing content in strategic ways that save time and build momentum.

WRITE AND RECEIVE

The Productive Writer is receptive. She pays attention. She sees herself in her world and her world in herself. She learns the names of things and invents the names of others. She is both seeking and satisfied, grounded at center and trained to the peripheries. With clarity and intention, she filters the steady swirl of sensory, interpersonal, and media information through the unique filter of her pen and page. She makes connections, records the resonance between known and believed. Collector of shells, scribe to wonder, she hones herself to a single star, both breathing in and giving off light.

SAVING ACORNS

It is unrealistic to expect to be seated comfortably at our desk with notebook open and pen poised every time an idea penetrates our force field. But it is realistic to develop fast, efficient systems for capturing the seed of an idea and storing it for later. Kim Stafford calls these little vessels of future writing "acorns." And so do I.

Here are some possible systems and strategies for being prepared for what comes so you can get it down quickly without disrupting the flow of your life. You may find one system works or that a mix of strategies serves your needs, depending on when inspiration hits.

Index Cards

This old-school tool is one of my favorites because it's easy to use and I am comforted by seeing my ideas in my own handwriting. I stash index cards where I sleep, work, eat, and travel. So any time I have an idea, there's a fast and easy way to write it down.

Voice Recorder

Voice recorders are faster than writing and becoming rapidly more accessible. Your cell phone is even likely to have one. Just keep in mind that (unless you're using voice recognition software) there's a transcription step that involves committing your spoken notes to paper.

Notebook

For years I did my freewriting in plain, cheap notebooks so I wouldn't feel pressure to write "important" stuff. These days, I prefer prettier, more substantial journals, but I keep the same deal with myself: Don't be too precious with 'em. Just let 'er rip. At a workshop a few years ago, Susan G. Wooldridge shared some of her notebooks that had flowers and wrappers and the multi-textured and -colored evidence of her life pasted in among the words. If a notebook appeals to you, the important

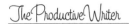

thing is to make sure you're comfortable with and likely to write in whatever style or format you choose.

Digital Notes

Your cell phone, PDA, and/or computer are all great places to type up a fleeting thought, depending on where you are and which is proximate.

Sticky Notes

Sticky notes are a useful way to capture something fast and stick it somewhere prominent. Some folks enjoy digital sticky notes, but I find that they get buried behind what I am working on.

Whiteboard

If positioned proximate to your moments of genius, whiteboards can be a great temporary home for a fleeting idea.

In-Box (and Then a Final Landing Place)

Toss whatever acorns you've collected on loose paper or small media in your in-box. Transcribe 'em into a computer document or notebook when you need a break, or store them in a special acorn receptacle, such as a box, drawer, or paper file folder, to keep your bounty safe.

Computer Document

I have a single computer document titled "Acorns," where I type all ideas that need to land somewhere. I always type my most recent idea at the top of the document.

DARLINGS: RESCUES FROM THE CUTTING FLOOR

Darlings is a term I've been using for so long that I don't remember its inception. I use it for both my business writing and my creative writing. If a word or line or stanza that I'm attached to in a poem just doesn't belong in this particular poem, it gets cataloged in my darlings file. Much like the acorn file, darlings has a record of every rescue from the creative cutting floor I've made in recent years. Often I'll grab a line from here to start a new poem, or even pluck a stanza into something in the works to see what happens next.

With my business writing, the darlings document tends to be per project. If I am writing a website, for example, and I cut out two paragraphs, I save them in that client's darlings file. Often, a chunk of language that didn't belong in one facet of a given project can find its home in some other expression—either on another page of the website or in a brochure or e-mail or press release.

Darlings have liberated me to be a far more swift and spontaneous editor. I can take action without second-guessing myself too much, because nothing is ever really lost; it's just relocated to the darlings file, where I can always grab it again if I need it.

The main idea here is don't let good thinking (encapsulated in good writing) go to waste. Know where it is and how to find it so you have your arsenal of extras on hand when you need them.

BORN AGAIN: BREATHING NEW LIFE INTO OLD WRITING

The beauty of having a writing platform is that it creates a context of big-picture coherence to what you are doing. One piece of writing at a time, over a period of years, you are writing yourself toward a comprehensive, integrated, and multifaceted tome of information on a topic that you are passionate about. Through this process, one piece of writing becomes a foothold for the next, until you approach vistas you never before imagined possible.

Instead of starting from scratch each time you pitch an article, workshop, or class, you can build on the wealth of information you've already researched and written, while finding a new dimension to explore or a new audience to educate. Let's consider an example:

Choose a topic.

Let's say mine is "Crafting Content That Sells."

Define potential audiences.

- Writers
  - Selling books
  - Who want to earn a living writing marketing copy
  - Selling articles to magazines
- Entrepreneurs
  - Solopreneurs
  - Women entrepreneurs
  - Local
  - Global
- Organizations that support business development
  - Chamber of Commerce
  - Ecotrust
  - Mamapreneurs
- Organizations that support writers
  - Willamette Writers
  - Oregon Writers' Colony
  - Soapstone
  - Oregon State Poetry Association

Explore expressions.

I could educate each of these audiences, or the people they serve, on this topic in one of the following possible forms:

- Presentations and lectures
- How-to articles
- Personal essay articles
- E-books
- Classes
- Video chats
- Podcasts
- Conference calls
- Blog posts/guest blogging
- Anthology submissions
- Themed publication submission
- Classes and workshops

You can see that by simply matching one topic with its various audience and expression possibilities, there are dozens of ways to repurpose the valuable knowledge you've worked hard to cultivate.

To start developing "repurposing consciousness," ask yourself each time you write or teach or offer something: To whom and how might I offer this topic next? Then take that step. And the next. And the next.

BUILD ON SUCCESS: REPEAT AND REFINE WHAT WORKS

When you do something that works in your writing life, do it again. In fact, make a point of seeking out opportunities to repeat and build on successes so you can use the momentum to fuel continued success. Whether it's a promotional strategy, a procrastination buster, a revision technique, or a craft insight, if it worked, use it whenever you can.

Templates Are a Writer's Best Friend

The more you can easily copy, paste, and modify something that served you well once, the more efficient and effective you will be. For example, I use templates to quickly create things like invoices, bids, contracts, press releases, queries, cover letters—anything I routinely use in the course of my writing life.

This is an easy system to establish and maintain. Simply create a "template" folder that's accessible in your computer and add templates to it as you go. Every time you need to create something new, reference your templates to see if you have a starting point to work with. Over time, you will likely have more targeted versions of these templates that you can organize by type of project, client, industry, publication, region, year, or whatever makes sense to most easily find what you need, when you need it.

Chapter 6

REINVENTING YOUR RELATIONSHIP WITH TIME

THE UNIVERSAL CHORUS OF COMPLAINT FROM WRITERS OF all stripes seems to be: not enough time. In this chapter, we're going to investigate how our relationship with time is moving us forward and holding us back. Then, in chapter seven, we'll get down to the nitty-gritty details of scheduling and planning.

TIME IS A LEVEL PLAYING FIELD

We all get the same twenty-four hours in a day. What you do with yours is up to you. You may believe that you have "no time," but the fact is, you have just as much time as anyone else. What varies for every writer is our unique mix of work and family responsibilities, financial commitments, sleep requirements, physical and emotional space for writing, and perhaps most importantly, our ability and willingness to prioritize writing in this mix.

Writers make time for writing. And everyone does it her own way. Your job is to find your way.

CONSCIOUSNESS IS THE FIRST STEP TOWARD CHANGE

Because I don't know you, I can't tell you exactly how you can make time for writing, but I assure you that you can. I can also tell you that your relationship with time is far more subjective than you might imagine. The best way to get a handle on how much authority you actually have over your time is to start becoming aware of how you are spending it. Chapter seven offers a friendly time-tracking method designed to give you a snapshot of your daily and weekly patterns.

Pay attention to how you're investing your time today, and you'll develop a clear picture of the mix of mandatory and voluntary activities that shape your days. Once you become conscious that your relationship with time is not something that happens *to you* but a dynamic orchestrated *by you* through dozens of large and small choices you make every day, you can evaluate if you would like to choose to continue the pattern you are in, or to create a new one.

HONOR YOUR RHYTHMS

Honor your biorhythms by planning your writing time for the part of the day you're most capable of doing it. For example, my friend Chloe De Segonzac just wrote to say that she's learned that waking up at 6:00 A.M. to write an important sex scene is not the way to go for her. It's hard to feel *steamy* when she's overwhelmed with *sleepy*.

I'm restless in the mornings and do my most focused work later in the day. Because I am fortunate to work for myself, from home, I have the flexibility to shape my time in a way that works for me. My schedule is always fluxing to accommodate changing workflow and family needs, but these days it generally looks something like this:

I'm with my young son until the late morning or midday, at which point someone else in the house cares for him. Once I put on my work hat, I'll participate in any client calls or meetings, business development opportunities, and such during the early hours of the day. Often I will do a big chunk of client writing or project management during the early part of the day as well. When I'm teaching, I find that I am able to focus and respond to student work very well at any time of the day. So I'll start this early, too. Nonfiction books and poetry and essays and everything that is being generated from the depths of my being and written onto the page generally happen in the evenings after my son is asleep.

Having transitioned from college directly to a series of office jobs, I had no idea what my biorhythms for different kinds of work were until I attended graduate school, where I had the flexibility to experiment with the various elements of my schedule. Chances are good that you've been in whatever life rhythm you're currently in for a good long while. This means you may not have any idea what might work best for you. Get ready to find out!

Define Your Prime Time

This is your invitation to start experimenting with your own sense of prime writing time. Right now. Does your cup overflow with imagery with that first coffee on the drive into work, or are you tapping the revelation vein at two in the morning when you can prowl in the shadows? Or maybe you're an "anytime is fine for me" kind of writer.

Do you need a six-hour chunk of uninterrupted time to really hit your stride, or can you make good progress during lunch break, standing in line at the post office, and waiting for your dentist appointment? How can you create more of the time-of-day and time-to-work intervals suited to your writing rhythms? No one can answer these questions but you, and even you may not have an informed answer yet. But soon, if you commit to finding out, you will.

Work With What You Have

I have just implored you to define your ideal writing times and patterns. And I meant it. But now, with equal emphasis, I would like to insist that you dig deep to define the scope of what's possible right this very minute.

Today, I am able to shape my workdays. But for many years, I was not. Despite the fact that it was not optimal for me to have my butt-in-chair in the morning (and it absolutely withered my soul to be in an office), there I was doing exactly that—sitting at a desk from 8:30 A.M. until at least 6:00 P.M. So, I made the best of it and worked with the margins I had. I carried a notebook when walking my dog in the mornings. I took public transportation to and from work and read and wrote as I bumped along into the shoulders of strangers. I spent weekend late afternoons alone in cafés reading and scribbling in note-books. I went to live music cafés in the evenings, in my pajamas, and while the people around me drank beer and sloshed about in time to the music, I filled pages with music coming through me in words.

In short, I refused to let a meaningless, demanding job deplete my creative stores. I insisted that my heart stay open to poetry and wrote myself awake every time my muse started to wander off looking for someone more reliable to haunt. I made writing my "everything else" around work, blended it with eating and entertainment and social time and care of my animals, and felt integrated, inspired, whole.

What are you doing right now to make the most of the time you do have, even if it's not your prime time? Start there, and experiment with how you might do a little more of it, and then a little more.

YOU HAVE THE REST OF YOUR LIFE

My computer monitor looks like a root system for sticky notes; it has become host to the layers and layers of pastel-posted ideas and to-dos that I scribble and stick as they flit through my mind while working. The accumulation of such notes creates a feeling of clutter, but more uncomfortably a sinking feeling that there will simply not be enough hours in my life to accomplish everything I want to do. But I know better.

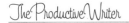

Several years ago, I took a workshop called "Falling Awake" with Dave Ellis. One of the preliminary assignments we were asked to do to prepare for the class was to chart out our major life goals for each area of our life in five-year segments. I defined my major areas as: health, finances, family, work, spirituality, and writing. And I brainstormed a mighty comprehensive list in each area.

I was thirty-four years old and single at the time. Based on longevity of my family members, I estimated that I'd be alive with my thinking cap on until at least age eighty-five. This gave me ten, five-year sets of time.

I dove into this exercise and was intently focused on plotting out conservatively realistic deadlines for my overwhelming list of goals throughout a fifty-year time spread when suddenly I came up empty-handed. Having arrived at the thirty-fifth year in this chart—age seventy—I had run out of goals. Everything I could possibly imagine that I might want to do in my life was accomplished. Imagine that! And I still had fifteen years to work with, give or take the unpredictable bargain of mortality.

So, I scrawled across the final fifteen-year segment in my most bawdy script: "Mourns death of older husband for some years before falling wildly and unexpectedly in love with a younger man."

What would life be like if you felt assured that there was plenty of time for every writing goal (and every life goal) on your dance card? What would you write (or not write) with fifteen gift years?

Make a "Rest-of-My-Life Plan" and Plot Your Possibilities

The common wisdom is, "Live like you're going to die tomorrow." My variation on this theme for writers is, "Write like you have the rest of your life ahead of you." And make your own rest-of-my-life plan to help you conceive the general shape and scope of what is possible.

With this big picture of your future sprawling out before you in measurable increments, you'll know far better whether you're aiming too high or leaving a purposeless decade or two dangling.

Don't worry, this plan isn't fixed in stone. So much happens in life that we can neither predict nor control. This is simply a way to estimate your capacity to inhabit the time you are given with the intentions you have chosen (and articulated clearly in chapters one and four). It's just another way of reassuring yourself that you have all day.

PROCRASTINATE PRODUCTIVELY

So you don't feel like writing. Or you're stuck on something and can't go any further right now. Or you're too tired or broke or can't find your pink slipper. Okay. You are excused. I don't do that stern school-teacher, butt-in-chair guilt trip. In fact, I've sworn off guilt trips altogether. So how, you may wonder, is this woman going to convince me to keep up all of that good, earnest writing work? She's not.

What I have come to trust from more than a decade of firsthand experience is that when we feel backed into a corner, we will rebel. So the more we try to force ourselves to write, the more we will resist, the less we will write, and the more frustrated and despairing we will become.

I would like to propose an alternative to this cat-and-mouse loop: Waste time well. If you do things that need doing—that you're actually in the mood to do—even procrastination can be productive. One of the things you'll start to learn over time is your rhythm for settling down to make stuff happen and the times when you need to rearrange your bulletin board a few times and eat lots of cookies.

Build Wasted Time Into Your Schedule

You probably know yourself pretty well by now. If you were the kid who had your term paper finished two weeks early, you're likely to be delivering ahead of your deadlines today. And if you needed the adrenaline rush of the all-nighter to crank out an entire thingamajig the night before it was due, chances are good that you possess a very high-end coffee machine to help you keep up the good work.

I happen to be a "waste-time-while-fearing-that-I-can't-do-it" type. Always have been. No matter how many thousands of times in my life I have proven this fear incontrovertibly wrong, it persists with its own independent logic and food supply. What I have learned to do is simply accept that this is going to be part of my process, not take it so seriously, and simply build the freak-out into my making-it-happen schedule.

When I signed my first book contract, I planned for a month of floundering, and I executed this step in the schedule fabulously well. I spent that month freaking out about not being smart enough, capable enough, worthy enough to write a book, while gobbling up multiple episodes of *Six Feet Under* on DVD every night. Suffice it to say that within about six weeks or so, I was stuffed uncomfortably full of death and dysfunction, and felt ready to shift gears.

Do you put obstacles in your own way when it comes to writing? How might you plan to accommodate your own resistance in a way that lets it think it is winning while burning out its fuse?

TOP TEN TIME-WASTING STRATEGIES

When you're not in a go-get-'em writing mode, the most important thing to do is keep your creative engine warm and running. The following list of possibilities is designed to help you keep your head in the game by doing things that indirectly benefit your writing life and can quickly create a feeling of either relaxation or reward.

1. **WRITE A BLOG POST.** Reinforce your expertise while doing a little fun, informal writing.

2. **VISIT YOUR ONLINE COMMUNITY.** Take a five-minute coffee break with other writers on Facebook and Twitter. Let their good news, struggles, questions, and insights percolate through you; chime

in here and there. Notice any seeds of new ideas, projects, or collaborations taking shape in your peripheral vision.

3. **MAKE ORDER.** Sort and purge your in-box. Vacuum or do dishes or fold laundry. You can improve beauty and order around you while resetting whatever brain pretzel you may be locked in.

4. **STAND UP AND STRETCH.** It's far easier to keep butt-in-chair if blood is flowing to it!

5. **DO YOUR DUE DILIGENCE.** Enter your business expense data into QuickBooks or pay bills.

6. **GET PREPARED.** Update your to-do list.

7. **EMPTY YOUR MIND.** A quick, three-minute meditation can settle your stirred waters so you can see clearly again.

8. **MANAGE YOUR CONTACTS.** Add business cards and other contact information you've collected recently into your contact database, sorting and categorizing appropriately by type of audience (students, colleagues, newsletter subscribers, etc.).

9. **SHARE THE WEALTH.** Visit a few favorite blogs or websites and tweet about your findings.

10. **CALL YOUR MOTHER.** (But don't open the mail while you talk; she won't like that.)

TAKE A TIME-OUT

I believe in signs. That's why, when my ten-month-old son pulled the book *Sabbath: Restoring the Sacred Rhythm of Rest* by Wayne Muller off the shelf for the third time, I decided it was time to read it.

Lo and behold, on that fateful Saturday, I took a day off from my computer. When my son Theo napped, I napped. Our family took a leisurely trip to the pool. My husband and I cooked a meal together. I felt like a human *being* instead of a human *doing*.

Muller credits Brother David Steindl-Rast for reminding us that the Chinese pictograph for *busy* is composed of two characters: heart and killing. This stopped me in my tracks. I, like almost everyone I know, am chronically, overwhelmingly busy. Muller proposes that a day of rest gives us the replenishment we need to live our lives well. To solve our problems creatively. To nourish our hearts—and in our case, dear reader, our writing.

That day of Sabbath was such a success that my husband and I committed to a family Sabbath every Saturday in which all work comes to a halt and the family simply relaxes, enjoys each other, and follows the threads of curiosity and delight wherever they might lead us.

The good news for all of us overachievers is that slowing down actually produces more: work, joy, equilibrium, love. I wonder if rest may be all we need to replenish our creative wells when they run dry.

HONOR YOUR TIME, SO THAT OTHERS CAN

Let's do some expectation setting here: No one in your family or community of friends is likely to have any idea what your writing life is all about. It's not that they won't want to support you; it's just that they won't know how.

Years ago, when I was employed as a writer on a marketing team for a company, the woman whose job it was to track and ship inventory reported me to my boss. According to her, I was "just sitting at my desk, staring out the window and doing nothing all day." The reality was that I was producing newsletters, articles, and brochures at an unprecedented rate and speed. And the other reality is that people who don't write don't necessarily understand that there is often reading, thinking, and rumination involved in the writing process—and this may not look like much to the casual observer.

People who don't write may not be able to imagine that you really and truly want to be in the closet with the door shut for three hours without talking to anyone. When you leave for that desperately anticipated writing retreat, don't take it personally when everyone you know wants to "come on vacation" with you.

The good news is that everyone who loves you can and will learn about your writing life if you are willing to teach them—and hold the line for yourself. All you need to worry about is being clear about the time you need and asking the people close to you for support in respecting that time. Like any limit setting, you are likely to be tested for a while.

I'd suggest adding to your arsenal this phrase, delivered with a smile: "Sure, I'd be happy to do [whatever has been requested] at [time] when I'm finished my writing. I'll see you then!" They might protest, but you can simply close the door and emerge at the time you have promised. I know you can. And the more practice you have with this, the easier it will get for you and everyone around you.

WE ARE NOT GIVEN TIME TO WRITE; WE TAKE IT

I remember as a young person reading somewhere that parents don't give you independence; you have to take it. I think that same premise holds true for establishing oneself as a writer. When you decide to write, the universe does not say, "How wonderful that you fancy yourself a writer, I'll give you three hours off of your job every day so you can fulfill your destiny." The reality is that it's up to you to create your writing time, to claim it, as if your blustery, teenage know-it-all self's future depends on it.

Chapter 7

SCHEDULING TIME AND TASKS

VISION WITHOUT ACTION IS A DAYDREAM. ACTION without vision is a nightmare."

—*Japanese proverb*

The Productive Writer makes the most of his time by:

- Knowing, tracking, and meeting deadlines.
- Measuring and monitoring how time is spent during the day.
- Learning how much time tasks take, and adapting accordingly.
- Making schedules to confirm that goals are achievable and to plot a course toward achieving them.
- Using the right systems for the most efficient scheduling.

The most disheartening place to be and feel as a writer is stuck. And the most possible place to be is in motion—moving toward our goals. At every turn, we have a choice in how we negotiate the demands of our lives with our own expectations for our writing practice. And no one is better equipped to help you navigate such challenges than you.

MANAGING DEADLINES

As a teenager, I slept so heavily that I would set three different alarms to wake up for school in the morning. The first alarm was on my nightstand. The one that rang second was on my dresser (which was close to the bed). The third and final alarm was all the way across the room. I had to get physically out of bed to reach it.

As you're establishing good deadline habits, you might want to set yourself up with the equivalent of these three alarms, exaggerating your deadline and time-management awareness to ensure that you don't miss anything important—especially if you have multiple projects going with a range of unrelated deadlines. Why? Because honoring your deadlines is respectful to yourself and the people you're working with. Meeting deadlines will give you and your colleagues, clients, editors, and publishers confidence in your ability to follow through. That's the kind of writer who gets hired a second time.

This chapter will introduce systems and strategies that can help you stay on task, deliver on time, and translate goals into accomplishments.

Schedules Are Windows Into the Possible

You may or may not be a "perform to a schedule" type of writer. Largely, this will depend on who you are, how you write, and what you're writing. For example, if you are writing poetry, there's a good chance that you're scratching your head about this suggestion. But if you've promised a business that they'll have an entire website worth of content in three weeks, you (and the client) will be well served knowing exactly how you're going to get there.

No matter what type of writing you're doing, whether there is an external deadline or not, a schedule can help. I have come to appreciate schedules as little maps of the possible to guide us in the deep and sometimes overwhelming waters of time. When I have a big project (let's say a book) and a somewhat long-term timeline (let's say six months) and some other significant work and family commitments, the fact of the matter is that I need to see where and how the writing time for the book is going to fit into my life. So I make a treasure map for arriving at the doorstep of this finished book on the date promised. When taken out of its romantic mood lighting, this map is simply a schedule.

What I mean by a schedule, for something like a book, is that I set both targets and timing. Let's say the book has twenty chapters, and I plan to write one chapter per week over the course of twenty weeks, then spend the last four weeks revising. I'd block off in my computer calendar the hours I expect to spend writing that chapter each week. For me, the greatest value of this process is having proof that there are actually enough hours in my life to accomplish what I have set out to do.

When I see those orange blocks of "write book" time floating through the days and nights of my computer calendar, a sense of calm comes over me. I can see my path of progress; I can trust it will get done. And even if I don't choose to stick to the schedule in a given week, or ever, I still have that visual map of how my current life could shift to accommodate something new—and a general sense of what will be required of me to make that happen. And that lends confidence and comfort as I enter the unknown.

Get ready to choose the time-management tools that work for you, track and understand how you're spending your time today, and chart out a week of work to discover what is possible.

USE THE RIGHT TIME-MANAGEMENT TOOLS

Following are some suggestions for a range of different approaches to time keeping and deadline management. Some are visual, some are interactive, some are high-level, and some are drilled down. Whatever your time-management style is, chances are good that you'll find something that works for you. I generally use a mix of all of these to fulfill various needs, to appeal to the various facets of my brain and personality, and because I hate to miss a deadline or fall behind.

Daily Deadlines: Whiteboards

A month-at-a-glance whiteboard calendar (with dry erase markers) can help you stay on top of key events and deadlines happening in any given month by:

- Understanding the big picture of what you're striving for and what you've committed to at any given time.
- Ensuring that all deliverables, deadlines, and public appearances stay in the forefront of your mind.
- Determining how much bandwidth you have to take on new work at any given time.
- Setting your performance priorities for any given day and week
- Pacing yourself appropriately to meet deadlines or goals on time without distress.

I use mine with color coding, so at a glance I can get a picture of the textures of commitment for any given day, week, and month. For example:

RED: client, editorial, and teaching deadlines and events

BLUE: personal commitments such as social engagements, houseguests, family travel, doctor's appointments

GREEN: literary commitments such as readings, lectures, classes, workshops I am leading or attending

What does your system look like?

The Panoramic Picture: Annual Calendar

For a year or two at a glance, I recommend using a write-on-wipe-off annual wall calendar. I'm talking about one that stands as tall as you do and has enough space in each day's square to write the most significant event happening or due that day. I like to think of mine as a patchwork quilt, where I piece together my own pattern of work, family, personal development, and rest. You can capture and plan the big picture of your writing life by recording:

- Conferences
- Vacation and other travel
- High-level work deadlines
- Teaching and speaking commitments
- Family events and vacations

With this panoramic view of your commitments, you can see everything on your plate across the rolling hills of many months. This helps you more easily plan for and monitor ongoing goals, such as making one public appearance every month or meeting a long-term deadline.

Instant Access: Computer Calendar

A computer calendar can include great detail about what's happening every day. This is where I track the hour-by-hour, nitty-gritty action items of what I expect to accomplish in a day. You can:

- Make a visual map of how a goal will be accomplished by designating chunks of work time.
- Easily track deadlines, meetings, birthdays, and other events.
- View history of work and plan ahead with automatic search and entry functions.
- Sync with a mobile phone or PDA and have your calendar with you anywhere, anytime.

Shared Calendars With Colleagues or Family: Google Calendar

Nothing says *I value your time* like a shared calendar where events, commitments, and deadlines can be viewed and updated by everyone involved, at any time. Businesses typically use a program like Microsoft Outlook for this; if you're working independently, Google calendar is a great (and free) way to go. Use it to:

- Plan and track calls, meetings, and vacations with colleagues.
- Know when the family car is available for work meetings.
- Arrange vacations that accommodate everyone's schedule.
- Facilitate child care and event planning with family and babysitters.
- Track writing or critique group meetings or other literary events shared by a particular community.
- View your own key dates and deadlines from any computer.

TIME TRACKING: PLANNING AND BILLING FOR YOUR TIME

As a writing professional, it is critical to track your time. Why? Because you need to know how long it takes you to write what you write. To accurately bid on a business writing project, for example, you need to know how long you will spend writing to ensure you are paid fairly. And when you are considering accepting that 1,000-word freelance article gig, it is important to know if the pay being offered translates to $1.00 per word or $.01 per word for the time you'll spend writing it.

Whether you are employed as a staff editor or independently writing a nonfiction book, freelance articles, poems, or fiction of any length, it's good to know how much time it takes you to write—and to understand the fluctuations in timing for related types of work. And whether you are billing clients for it, getting paid by editors or publishers for it, or simply learning how to track and boost your performance, having a

handle on what you do with time is critical to your sense of confidence and your ability to deliver on promises—to yourself and others.

How to Use a Time-Tracking Log

To get a handle on how I spend time, I use a daily time sheet, which is a table that I create, print out, and fill out by hand. I keep one for each project, as well as one that illustrates each day's big picture.

 Download a sample daily time log at
WritersDigest.com/article/productive-writer-downloads.

It may seem daunting at first to track how you spend your time. But it's actually quite easy to do, and very quickly it will become second nature. You can experiment with computer programs such as TimeSlice that will let you automate time tracking on a computer, but these are typically set up for someone to clock in and out throughout the day while at his computer. If you are juggling all kinds of other things that do not involve sitting at your desk for long stretches of time, this is probably not a time-management technology for you.

Once you have a clear picture of how you've spent every hour of every day for a week or two or three, you'll know:

- How much time it takes you to do the work you're doing.
- How much time you're wasting.
- How much time you'd like to reassign to your writing practice.

With knowledge comes choice: to repeat a pattern or choose a new one.

ALIGN GOALS, TASKS, AND TIME

In chapter one, you defined your writing goals. In chapter four, you practiced prioritizing tasks and breaking them down into manageable steps. In chapter six, you got clear about your preferred writing rhythm times. And on the previous pages, you learned how much time it takes to do the things you do in your writing and your life.

Now think about how all of these puzzle pieces might shake out to the pretty picture of an actual schedule. Consider two very general possibilities: the life of the employee who writes in the margins and the life of a full-time writer. Both scenarios present their own challenges. Whether you're planning your writing schedule around your day job or planning around other responsibilities such as parenting, assigning specific time slots can help you manage your writing-related tasks.

 Examples of weekly schedules for part-time and full-time writers are available for download at WritersDigest.com/article/productive-writer-downloads.

Advantages of Pre-scheduling Your Days and Weeks

- You can literally plot out your writing goals in chunks of time.
- You can reserve time for each important part of your life; this prevents your schedule from filling up with activities that are not in service to these priorities.
- You can prove to yourself that there is, indeed, time for what matters to you when you plan for writing and honor that plan.

 Download your own weekly schedule template at WritersDigest.com/article/productive-writer-downloads.

Even if you don't think you're a schedule kind of person, I invite you to try it for a month and see what happens. Maybe you'll confirm that this kind of left-brain rigor is just not your cup of tea. Or maybe you'll enjoy seeing hard proof of what is possible and what you are accomplishing every day and every week. You'll never know until you try.

Chapter 8

WHEN STRIVING FOR PRODUCTIVITY, IT'S EASY TO FOCUS on output and forget about the requisite input that can keep the well full, gears oiled, and all the other clichés chugging right along. Inspiration is not something that happens to us. It is something we seek, cultivate, aspire to, and align ourselves with. It is the writer's way.

Writing is the love affair you have with yourself that readers happen to overhear.

RITUAL AND ANTIRITUAL

> The hollow you carve for writing is to be praised. You have to be particular. The chair, the paper, the view you choose, that will be some of your best work. Do you drink? Drink from a chalice. Do you wear a shirt? Do not wear just any shirt, wear the prosperous one, trust me on this. If poverty is your ideal, by all means be the poorest and wallow in owning nothingness. And your thoughts, give them away as well, let nothing belong to you if that is your Eden. Whatever that beauty is, invite yourself in its center, as guest of honor.

Or, be as the pump in a spring, primed and r
When your flow fades —nothing is forever—then
slightly, and dig yourself a new well."

—GRÉGOIRE VION, *award-winning poet*
and illustrator

What Grégoire is speaking to here are two sides of the same process coin: ritual and anti-ritual. Rituals can serve a writer extremely well, until they don't.

When we ritualize our way of approaching our thoughts, our themes, and our work, we can establish a powerful way to connect with our genius. We train ourselves to quickly and easily enter the zone, then stay there for as long as we need to be successful.

For example, I have come to depend on taking a family dog walk while drinking a chai tea latte to kick-start my day. This is the time that I shake off the evening before and rev up my engines for all that lies ahead. I love to breathe fresh air, get wet (it's almost always raining here in Portland), sing songs to my son, and watch my dogs frolic and wrestle as the primer for all that is to color the rest of my day.

Flip that coin and you'll find that a groove traveled enough times has a tendency to become a rut. The time will likely come when the same old process yields the same old writing. That's when it's time to experiment with a new writing ritual. Lately, I'm waking up at 5:00 A.M. and writing until my son rises at 7:00 A.M. I've never been much of a morning writer, but I'm finding that the silence yields some clear insights and precise writing. I like that my first thinking of the day is going to my own projects, even if clients' objectives will occupy my mind share for the better part of the rest of the day.

All of this to say: Keep that shovel close at hand, and when the chalice stops serving up wine, you'll know it's time to start digging.

INSPIRATION WORKOUT

It is rumored that at a party, author Margaret Atwood was speaking to a neurosurgeon who mentioned that he had just retired and was considering writing a book, to which she replied, "What a coincidence! I was thinking of becoming a neurosurgeon when I retire."

I've always appreciated this little snippet of dialogue for its witty innuendo about the rigors of the writing life. Just as you are not likely to wake up one morning and run the New York City marathon without training for it, you can't expect that cartoon light bulb to come on over your head the moment you sit down to write if you don't practice. So grab whatever props make you feel writerly, then start stretching and get ready for your inspiration workout.

Reading Regimen

At any one time, I'd recommend reading a mix of books concurrently, including at least a few of the following topics:

- Developing your craft
- Inspiration/fun (unrelated to your genre)
- A book you admire in your genre
- Marketing and/or selling your work
- Nonfiction on a topic that interests you

This is what works for me. What is your ideal mix of reading material to keep you inspired, informed, and awake to possibility?

LISTENING REGIMEN

Listen to people you admire read from their work or talk about what they do. This is one of my favorite forms of rocket fuel for my own sense of possibility—both for my writing craft and my writing career. If you don't have easily accessible literary events in your community, or you don't have the flexibility to attend them, tune in online. In just a few clicks, you can tap a wealth of videos and podcasts of writers of every stripe reading, lecturing, giving interviews, and more.

COMMUNITY-BUILDING REGIMEN

Writers need some very basic things: some scraps of writing time, pieced together into great tapestries; a pen and paper; and a sense of community. Yes, even you, who started writing in the first place because you are an introvert who prefers your own company, need a tribe. Books themselves offer one of the most nourishing opportunities for community. When we recognize ourselves in the writing of others, or through their writing get a glimpse of a newly revealed facet of the universal human condition, this is tribe.

But books are a one-way relationship. The companionship of other writers can afford dialogue and a shared exploration and witnessing of what is possible in the writing life.

In an article titled "Chalk and Cheese" in *Metroactive Books*, author Jordan E. Rosenfeld explores the relationship between poets Dana Gioia and Kay Ryan:

> "For most of the world," Ryan reflects, "writing, especially writing poetry, might be a nice hobby or recreation, but not a primary passion or the deepest engagement with life. It's wonderful to have someone as a friend for whom it is essential and central."

Having friends to learn with and from, who are intimately engaged with the unique opportunities and challenges of the writing life, is something that I wish for every writer. And I hope you will make it a priority to seek out such people along the way. If you do not have access to a community of writers where you live, there are plenty of

communities to tap online that give you access to people around the world who share your passions and proclivities.

Everything you strive for will feel more possible and be more productive and pleasurable in the company of someone who cares about you and has similar aspirations. Plus, you are likely to understand more about what is possible in your craft and in the realm of publishing as you witness the choices and successes of your community. (A word of caution: Writing communities are built on relationships, and the quality of your experience depends on the quality of those relationships. If you're participating in a group that leaves you feeling discouraged, inferior, or unwelcome, move on until you find one that brings out your best.)

PERSONAL AND PROFESSIONAL DEVELOPMENT REGIMEN

Plants need sun and water to grow. What do writers need? In addition to a keen appreciation for sun and water, this writer has found that a focused and regular approach to professional development keeps me growing. Classes, workshops, and conferences are great ways to bring together some of the opportunities I've proposed for filling your cup. You can meet other like-minded writers who may eventually become friends and colleagues, listen to and learn from people whose writing and expertise you respect, and learn new skills—everything from craft to publishing to promotion—that can help give you a sense of the bigger picture of where you'd like to steer your writing craft.

When I wanted to learn more about what was possible in my writing life beyond my poetry and the marketing communications writing I was doing professionally, I set out to learn about the realm of nonfiction writing. Essays, magazine articles, books. In the margins of a full-time life, I took it slow and stayed steady, with approximately one to two classes and one conference per year. I made sure I could afford both the time and the money to pursue these opportunities, and committed to putting into practice what I learned along the way.

I encourage you to seek out ways to learn more about the dimensions of your writing life you are most excited about developing. Don't forget to pace yourself so you have time to actually do the work you are learning about. And if you don't have the funds for classes or conferences, check out a stack of books on writing, publishing, or promoting from your local library or find the blogs that offer valuable guidance from successful writers who are in the trenches you intend to someday occupy. And when all else fails, remember that your life itself is the greatest learning laboratory of all.

EMBRACE YOUR GENIUS (BUT DON'T CONFUSE IT FOR YOU)

When Elizabeth Gilbert, author of *Eat Pray Love,* came to Portland, Oregon, a few years ago, she reminded us that in Ancient Greece and Ancient Rome, people did not attribute creativity to the person making art. Instead, it was believed that artists channeled creativity through divine spirits that choose us and live alongside us. In this framework of understanding, each artist (writers being artists) has a designated spirit or entity that is on call to assist with her work, peppering her with its brilliance basically whenever it is required. The Romans called this spirit "a genius." Then, during the Renaissance, the idea of "having a genius" began to move toward today's paradigm of "being a genius."

Gilbert proposed, and I agree, that we return to the entirely scientifically unsound possibility of "having a genius," that is, something outside of us that beams in those "aha" moments that seem to arrive out of nowhere, rather than "being a genius," a burden which she equates to swallowing the sun. Let me explain.

Having a Genius vs. Being a Genius

Gilbert gives a historical and sociological frame to something I have always instinctively believed to be true about the writing life: We writers are tapping the source—we are not the source. In a way, this is what

makes writing relational. We are not all we need. We need to be humble, grateful, and tuned in to what is being so generously provided for us.

I'm not saying that we don't have to work hard, but rather that we are training ourselves in the samurai sport of cosmic butterfly catching. We are developing our muscles and our receptivity, fine-tuning our nets, so that we are ready to receive what comes and translate it to the page.

Like a dance partner to the cosmos, we are cultivating the agility of mind, listening, and language to move with what comes through while holding the frame. We can't dance with a partner if we're all tangled up in each other's legs and arms.

For writers today, there are some real advantages to this concept of having a genius. Namely, it takes us off the hook from identifying so much with what we create. There is a little more emotional distance and breathing room between our work and our selves.

The Genius Is Not the Muse

Maybe the muse has a bad rap, but I have come to think of her as that fickle lover you can never count on to show up in a pinch, and one you would never want to leave alone with your best friend. So I propose that we invite the muse to contribute her expertise in starting those imagination brushfires, and turn to another archetype for keeping the coals burning steady and strong throughout those dark and cold writing nights.

This is where the genius comes in, as a kind of archetypal companion who is as dedicated to you and as invested in your success as a fairy godmother. And we get to be the singular recipient of her beneficence. Maybe this kills the romance of it all for you, but I've become a practical woman in my middle age, and I want a creative coconspirator who's going to stick around, stand in my corner, and keep me writing toward the most unlikely of miracles.

From Swallowing the Sun to Radiating Light

This past year, I've been touring the country talking to people about the life poetic, the topic of my most recent book. Generally at the beginning of the lecture, I ask three questions: "How many of you are writing poetry today?" (Folks raise their hands.) "And how many of you would like to be writing poetry but haven't started yet?" (Another show of hands.) "And who here once wrote poetry but then got happy?" Inevitably, a roar of laughter ripples through the room as listeners are caught off guard by this truth that occurs in their own writing practice, though they had never quite realized or articulated it. Generally, most of the room raises their hands.

It is a common assumption that writers are unhappy and unwell; we often even consciously or unconsciously expect it of ourselves. While our literary lexicon certainly has its share of tragic writers represented throughout the course of history, this genius I am proposing is not driven by mental illness, addiction, or self-sabotaging dysfunction. As I see it, The Suffering Writer is giving way to a new archetype that we are shaping together: The Productive Writer who cultivates his being such that he becomes hospitable to a sustainable life and writing practice that is attuned to possibility and hard-wired for prosperity. This is not to say that we Productive Writers are not without our struggles and challenges; only that they do not define us or our writing lives. The Productive Writer writes what she is called to write, pitches it intelligently and places it well, is paid fairly, makes a lasting and favorable impact with promotions and presentations, and lives an engaged, balanced, satisfying life.

Poet and memoirist Judith Barrington tells her students the following: "When your therapy is complete, that's when it's time to write the memoir." The Suffering Artist may swallow the sun, but the Productive Writer radiates light.

LEARNING TO TRUST THE FLOW

You have a genius and you have a life. Your job as a writer is to keep the two in balance, allowing them to feed each other without stripping each other bare. Once you have enough experience with welcoming your genius, both you and your genius can establish your reliability to each other. Then each of you can take a day off every now and then. If you trust it will be back, you won't drive yourself crazy trying to chase it. And if your genius trusts you are listening, it won't be working so hard to break through your resistance with attention-getting stunts that slow you down and eventually force you to listen.

While your job as a writer is to hone the instrument of your life to transmit the best possible writing, your job as a person is to honor and cultivate the balance and delight of your existence here on Earth. When writing is in service to our life, we are likely to be balanced and content. When our life is in service to our writing, it can feel like driving without breaks. Let me explain.

In Elizabeth Gilbert's TED (Technology, Entertainment, Design) presentation, she describes an interview with Tom Waits where he revealed that for most of his life, he struggled with his source of inspiration, felt captive to it, and let it boss him around every which way. Then, one day while driving on the freeway in LA, he heard a fragment of melody and got quite upset about wanting to capture it and not being able to do so. Next, something completely unprecedented happened. Waits looked up at the sky and is reported to have said something along the lines of: "Excuse me; can you not see that I am driving? If you really want to exist, come back at a more opportune moment. Otherwise, go bother Leonard Cohen."

I think this is a fine example of our relationship with the genius, like any relationship, being a two-way street. When we treat our genius with respect, we will be visited often. And when we set healthy limits

around our availability, our genius will learn to respect us, too. We may be surprised when the polite knocks start coming during "office hours" and other optimal times for receiving that whisper in our ear.

> ### My Genius Manifesto
>
> Genius, I appreciate how you have helped me to accomplish: _____
> _____. Today, I'd love your help with: _____
> My office hours are [time] _____ to [time] _____on _____
> [day(s) of the week]; let's get together then. I always welcome your new
> ideas! When I'm off duty, you can file ideas [where] _____. I'll
> have my [name your idea-capturing system, such as note cards, notebook,
> tape recorder, etc.] with me as much as possible and will be happy to get
> it all down when I can.

Naming Your Source

I'm not particularly invested in you buying into this "having a genius" paradigm, but I am invested in you coming up with a term and a context for yourself that makes sense to you and the way you work. Maybe you and the Oompa Loompas from Willy Wonka's chocolate factory are in cahoots. That's cool by me. Or maybe you and the muse have settled in for a long-term commitment. Terrific. It's also possible that you are accompaniment agnostic and you prefer to see yourself as the bootstrapping source of all that comes through you, without the support of any imaginary archetypes; fair enough. All I want for you is this: a context for working with yourself that is generous to you but not indulgent, gives you room to be human and make mistakes, and keeps you humble about it all—and most importantly, writing.

Chapter 9

PUTTING INFORMATION AT YOUR FINGERTIPS

FOR WRITERS, INFORMATION IS GOLD. THE MORE WE HAVE, the richer the possibilities for our writing and our lives. Throughout the day (and night), we need to access a vast range of information from an incredible array of sources, many of which are right in our own homes, offices, and computers.

The truth is, we're so used to being in our own way, tripping over our own bad organizational habits, that it's hard to even imagine what it might be like to effortlessly find the information we seek.

The truth is, it's possible to create an information system that is so synchronized with your thinking and intuition that you can put your finger on the pulse of whatever you need, the instant you need it.

Let's get started, shall we?

The Productive Writer puts information at her fingertips by:

- Organizing books in a relevant and manageable system.
- Staying on top of the in-box (and making fast decisions).
- Knowing what to save and what to toss.
- Maintaining simple, coherent paper filing and e-mail archiving systems.
- Using a clear and consistent file names and folder organization so documents are easy to find.
- Backing up her computer.

ROMANCING YOUR BOOKSHELF

If I may be so bold as to generalize: Writers love books. So, suffice it to say, many of us have many books. Far too many. How do we avoid straining and swaying under the weight of so much literary love? Use these tips so your books will remain a bounty, not a burden.

- **DESIGNATE A TYPE OF BOOK FOR EACH BOOKSHELF.** For example, I have separate shelves for writing reference books, teaching books, marketing books, fiction, creative process/inspiration … You get the idea.

- **ALPHABETIZE ACCORDING TO HOW YOU SEEK INFORMATION.** When you want to find a book, do you search by title or author name? Whatever your answer, that's how you should alphabetize your bookshelves. For example, I generally look for poetry books by searching for the poet's name. So I alphabetize those by author name. Whereas, I refer to writing reference books by title. So that's how I alphabetize that section of my shelf.

- **PUT WHAT YOU USE THE MOST IN REACH.** You don't want to be walking across the room or into another part of the house or office to get the dictionary if you're using it three times a day. Pay attention to the books you refer to regularly and make sure that section of your book storage is as close to you as possible. For example, my poetry collection does not reside in my office because I don't refer to it much while I'm working at my day job. Whereas, I keep my style guide, thesaurus, and promotion/marketing guides within an arm's reach of my desk.

- **HOUSE-TRAIN EVERY NEW BOOK.** When you bring a book home, find a place for it on your bookshelf immediately.

- **BEDSIDE TABLES. BATHTUBS. BEST FRIENDS' HOMES.** What do these three things have in common? Each could become a black hole for your books. The places where you spend time reading are the

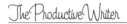

places where piles of books can collect. Every week or so, evaluate these piles and re-shelve everything that is not being read.

- **CORRAL THOSE NOTEBOOKS INTO A SINGLE SYSTEM.** It's time to round up those composition books and spiral-bound notebooks into a single easy-to-access holding pen.

  You can organize by time (month, year, or decade), by theme (morning pages, freewriting, journaling, love letters), or by function (plot development for Novel A, character development for Novel B). You can keep these orderly by inserting them in standing magazine holders designed for bookshelves. Or, if you no longer need to reference the notebooks on a regular basis, you can store them in a closet or weather-safe attic.

- **KEEP A LENDING LIBRARY.** When you loan out books, create a check-out log so you know what you've given away, to whom, and when. If you give something away for good, make note of that, too. Then you won't waste time searching for it the next time. You can even get pretty faceplate stickers that say, "From the library of … " to help friends remember that the book they're reading belongs to you.

- **CREATE A LIBRARY-QUALITY CATALOG.** If you want to get really high-tech (and community minded) with your book organization project, you can join LibraryThing, a cataloguing and social networking site for book lovers. Use this service both to create a library-quality catalog of your books and to connect with people who have common books in their libraries.

- **PRETEND YOU'RE IN COLLEGE FOR THE REST OF YOUR LIFE.** I learned a great skill in college: defiling books. And it's served me well ever since. When you own books, write in them. Underline, highlight, and make margin notes. It will help you make the information in the book your own. Plus, you'll be able to easily remember/reference your own experience of it if you return to the book later. If you read books digitally, such notations are particularly easy to make and reference.

- **THE LIBRARY IS YOUR FRIEND.** If you don't absolutely need to have a book at your beck and call for the rest of your life, borrow it instead of buying it. This is good for your budget, good for the environment, and good for your new commitment to clutter management. Make a special place on your bookshelf for borrowed books—from the library or friends.

- **REMEMBER THAT BOOKS CAN BE A TAX WRITE-OFF.** Record any legitimate expenses for books that inform your writing, marketing, education, or platform development.

- **MAKE NEW FRIENDS, BUT KEEP THE OLD.** At least once a year, let go of books that you've read, don't intend to read, and don't expect to need again. This will relieve some of your dead weight and make space for new ideas and information to enter your life.

- **GO DIGITAL.** Digital book readers and computer notepads offer an efficient way to put a great volume of information (such as an entire library of books) at your fingertips—and immediately read or reference whatever you are seeking at any time.

REIGN IN YOUR IN-BOX

Act Now, or Forever Hold Your Piles

Paper accumulates so fast, you'd think it had a will of its own. Following are some tips for teaching your paper piles to sit, stay, and fetch. It all begins with showing your in-box who's the boss.

The Art of the In-Box

- Designate an in-box that you can reach from where you sit to work.
- Your in-box should be the very first destination for all paper that comes your way.

- At least once a day, go through the stash and make an immediate decision about what needs to happen next with each piece of paper; then do it. This is the key to avoiding a paperwork pileup. The more you practice, the better you'll get.
- The action you take next will depend on the status of each item.

STATUS	ACTION
Don't want or need	Recycle

Action needs to be taken by you:
  • Payment owed
  • Save for later
  • Needs further attention/action
	Sort into the appropriate folder:
	  • Bills to be paid
	  • To be filed (you'll learn more about this on page 87)
	  • To do

Action needs to be taken by someone else	Move to out-box. Pass on the information to the appropriate person that same day.

SAVING PAPER

Making Sense of Your Stash–Then Making It Accessible

You've whittled out what needs to be saved from your in-box. Now it's time to tame your to-be-filed pile.

The only things that belong in a file cabinet are documents that don't exist anywhere else. For example, if you have a short story in your computer, there's no reason to print out an exact copy and take up space in your file drawer. However, if you have a hard copy of this story that a colleague, teacher, or editor marked up with handwritten feedback, you'll want to preserve that copy in a file cabinet.

What to File

- One-of-a-kind materials for which you don't have a soft (computer) copy, such as: brochures, memorabilia, catalogs, user's manuals, correspondence, warranties, menus

- Signed contracts and other legal paperwork
- Writing with handwritten edits or feedback
- Reviews and clips of your work
- Acceptance and rejection letters
- Drafts of your writing (only if they are not also saved on your computer)
- Financial and accounting records dating back at least five years (some say three years; I am conservative)

How to Find What You've Filed

- Clearly write the contents of each drawer in large, legible text so you'll know what's inside at a glance. (For example, I have file drawers labeled "personal," "client projects," and "creative writing.")
- Color code file folders if there are only two or three major categories. More than three categories just becomes a mess. (For example, my writing folders are red; clients are green; personal is blue.)
- Alphabetize your files. This is the fastest and easiest way to find a paper in a haystack.

System Maintenance

- **LOCATION, LOCATION, LOCATION.** Your file cabinet's proximity to you should be directly related to its frequency of use. If you're retrieving or filing information multiple times a day, it should be no more than a few steps from where you sit. If you use it once a month or less, the cabinet could be stored across the room, in a closet, or in another room entirely.

- **THE FILING 1-2-3.** Every time you're about to file something, ask yourself these three questions:

    1. *Will I need to refer to this again?* If yes, go to number 2; if no, toss.

2. *Do I have an electronic copy of this I could use instead?* If no, go to number 3; if yes, toss.

3. *Is there an existing file folder where this might belong?* If yes, file accordingly. If no, choose the color file folder—if any—that's appropriate for this type of document, write a name on it, and then file. If your file says "health," for example, make sure there's no file named "medical" that has the same information in it.

- **EVERYTHING I NEED TO KNOW ABOUT FILING I LEARNED IN KINDERGARTEN.** At the end of each day or session at your desk, make sure to return all files to their rightful, alphabetical place so they'll be there when you need them next time.

- **KNOW YOUR FILING STYLE.** My dear friend and longtime colleague Pamela Kim swears by those little labeling machines for creating perfectly uniform file folder name tags. I, on the other hand, prefer to look at my own handwriting. Do whatever works for you; just be consistent.

- **AVOID THE BLACK HOLE.** Every six months, do a purge of the cabinet to clear out everything you haven't used in the past six months. Toss what you can. Anything that you expect to need in the future (such as legal or financial documents) can be transitioned to a cardboard file storage box called a banker's box and moved into a safe and dry long-term storage space, such as an attic.

- **BEYOND THE FILE CABINET.** The file cabinet is one of many file storage and maintenance choices. You may also have file drawers in a credenza or built into your desk. Or you may prefer those little milk crates on wheels, accordion folders, or wire desk stands.

What you use is less important than how you use it. These are a few examples of how form might serve function for you:

FORM	FUNCTION
File storage boxes	Long-term storage that you may need to refer to every year at most.
File cabinet	Stuff you need access to anywhere from daily to monthly.
File drawer in your desk, at your feet, or somewhere in reach	Information you use most frequently; projects that are active now.
File stand on your desk	Everything in-the-works that you need visual and physical access to each time you sit down to work.

FILE NAMING CONVENTIONS

A Document by Another Name Would Still Be as Sweet (But Likely Lost)

You write a lot of great stuff. You want to be able to find it when you need it. The key to instant retrieval from that vast no-man's-land of the computer hard drive is to name your files the same way, every time. And to do so in a way that fits both your logic and the type of writing you're saving.

> **Three rules of naming computer documents:**
>
> 1. Keep file names as simple as possible.
> 2. Include enough detail about the project, date, or version to easily find the exact document you need, when you need it.
> 3. Choose a naming convention and be consistent with every name, every time.

The logic of file naming is simple. Ask yourself these questions:

- What will be the most obvious search terms I'd use for the file?
- What details will help me clarify if I've found the file I want?

For example, the key information I search by for my client work is: name of client, name of project, and date. (Much of my client work involves multiple revisions. The simplest way for me to manage version control is by date. I can easily see which was finished last and know that it is the most current and therefore accurate.)

Therefore, I name client files like so:

> NAME OF CLIENT + name of project + month/day/year:
> **CLIENTproject092210**

My husband wants everything he does organized first by date so he can easily find whatever is most current in his entire archive of documents. So his naming for the same file might be:

> Year/month/day + NAME OF CLIENT + name of project:
> **100922CLIENTproject**

Because I do different types of writing, I name some documents differently. For example, I name my poems by their title and version only. Because I could work on the same poem for a decade or more, date is far less relevant than being able to easily see which is the latest/greatest version:

> Alchemy v1
> Alchemy v2
> Alchemy v3

The trick is to name every poem using this same convention and every client file using the convention described above. With a consistent ritual, you'll know exactly what to do when you hit "save as," and you'll save so much more time when you can instantly retrieve what you're seeking.

FILE FOLDER ORGANIZATION

Hierarchy Has Its Place: In Your Documents Folder

Effective file naming will keep you in the Productive Writer race. Effective file folder naming and organizing will take you across the finish line. The key to an effective system is a meaningful hierarchy of information that is established through repetition.

Three Rules for Naming Computer File Folders:

1. Keep the main directory as simple, brief, and high-level as possible (with no more than ten folders.)
2. Create subfolders for every type of information within the larger category. (This is where it benefits you to be as detailed as possible.)
3. Be consistent. All subfolders for each category should be the same.

 Visit WritersDigest.com/article/productive-writer-downloads for examples of various work/life filing conventions.

E-MAIL EFFICIENCIES

Leave a Virtual Paper Trail—and Recall It in an Instant

Chances are, a good number of the promises you've made, edits you've received, and celebrations you've shared have happened in the ether. Whether it's for professional record keeping or personal nostalgia, you'll want easy access to your e-arsenal.

Tips for Effective E-Archiving:

- When you send an important e-mail, bcc yourself. Then you'll know for sure that the e-mail went out, and you'll have a record of receipt on file.
- Organize your e-mailboxes using a similar hierarchy to your computer file folders. (See page 87.)

- Do not have your e-mail automatically sorted into folders before you've read it. If it's not in front of you in your in-box, you are far less likely to read it.
- Empty your e-mail in-box every day. A backlog of unanswered e-mail will weigh you down.
- After responding to each e-mail, decide whether it needs to be deleted or saved. Act accordingly.
- Any e-mail you wish to save should be filed in the appropriate e-mailbox immediately.
- Review your e-mailboxes once every six months and purge everything you don't need.

Save an E-Mail When:

- You need a "paper" trail. (It proves that you or someone else did something, or it articulates a promise you or someone else made.)
- It includes information you'll need in the future.
- You can use it for promotion, inspiration, teaching, education, or community building.
- It makes you laugh, cry, or [insert desired feeling here].

USE IT; DON'T LOSE IT

> *Once, early in my career, I did a phone interview with an important and hard-to-reach person. Imagine my dismay when I discovered the next day that my office had been broken into and my tape recorder—with the interview on it—had been stolen. I had to call the source back and interview him again. Humiliating!*
>
> *Since then, I've had issues with low batteries and faulty microcassettes (I've since switched to a digital voice recorder). So every time I do an important phone interview, I type notes*

on my laptop in addition to recording it. That way, even if something goes wrong with the recorder, I've got most of the info typed up. Also, I immediately save a copy of the recording and the notes on a CD or flash drive, just in case."

—ABIGAIL GREEN, *freelance writer and editor*

How and Why to Back Up Your Computer

If you are like me, your computer serves as your brain's external hard drive. What you hold most precious (outside of your own life and the lives of your loved ones, of course) lives in that fickle piece of machinery that could quit at any moment without a word of notice. Are you prepared for that? If you're not, I want you to do two things right now:

1. Get a backup hard drive (I use a Lacie) with memory matching or exceeding your computer's; set it up to automatically back up your computer every day.

2. Subscribe to an off-site backup service (I use mozy.com), which will automatically back up your computer for you at regular intervals. Having your data backed up to a server that is not in your house means you're covered in the event of (God forbid) a robbery or a fire in which both your computer and hard drive are lost.

Neither is hard to do; both are relatively low in cost; the peace of mind you will experience is priceless.

Chapter 10

THERE'S NOTHING HARDER IN LIFE THAN TRANSITIONS. For most of us, being in-between is just plain uncomfortable. And the writing life is no different. Let's explore some ways to make transitions as smooth and welcoming as possible for ourselves.

FACING THE BLANK PAGE

> *The pages are still blank, but there is a miraculous feeling of the words being there, written in invisible ink and clamoring to become visible."*

—VLADIMIR NABOKOV

What is it that infuses Nabokov with this trust in the possibilities that await him on the blank page? I'd propose that the answer is experience. The more times we face the blank page with the expectation of the miracle awaiting us there, the more we are training ourselves to this inevitability. What if we were to commit to referencing this idea every time we start to panic about the writing unknowns that lie ahead?

From Zero to One

Making the leap from nothing to something is alchemy. An idea or word or image that never existed before in just-this-way appears and gets written down. As in any birth, you may experience turbulence as the unprecedented is taking shape and coming through, thrashing about for form and coherence and context. And if you keep at it, chaos and all, a kind of systemic order eventually stumbles into itself. There are feathers, yes. And the feathers start lining up and settling down into the bigger picture: wing. And then the aperture opens to include: bird. And then even more extraordinary: flock. Suddenly, you have written words that have given shape and meaning. You have birthed a bird and you know where it is going. You have traveled somewhere specific that your readers can follow.

ENTERING THE ZONE

We waste time because we don't know how to get our butt in the chair and get started. It can be quite confronting to face the blank page. Following are some suggestions for easing yourself into a rhythm of writing. I invite you to experiment with what appeals to you, repeat what works, and then try something else when it stops working. And if nothing on this list blows the cap off of your pen, by all means, sit down right now and brainstorm your own list of triggers. The point is, take charge, take action, and keep moving forward until a gear clicks and you find your way forward.

- **SWITCH GENRES.** Write a first-draft poem before diving into a larger fiction or nonfiction piece.
- **GET LOOSE.** Do some freewriting to loosen your arm, your mind, and your inner editor.
- **MINE YOUR ARCHIVES.** Review past freewriting for inspired ideas or language.
- **PLANT AN ACORN.** Scan through your "acorn" pages; see if anything grabs you (see chapter five for more detail).

- **DO YOUR DARLING DILIGENCE.** Consider "darling" files for threads you might like to pick up today (see chapter five).
- **DEFY DEFINITION.** Open the dictionary to a random page and read; choose a word from which your writing will unfold.
- **BE RANDOM.** Open any book of poems or fiction randomly and read one page. Find a line or a phrase or an idea you admire. Write about it, or start from there.
- **ACCEPT WHAT YOU ARE GIVEN.** Trade daily writing prompts with a friend; write from what you are given.
- **BURN KINDLING.** Keep an inspiration file of art, poems, quotes—whatever it is that calls to you as kindling for the fire of your imagination. Then sift through it when you need a spark.
- **ENGAGE YOUR LEFT BRAIN.** Research some topic that will inform a piece you are working on. Set a ten-minute time limit.
- **IMITATE WHAT YOU ADMIRE.** Read a piece of writing that you hold as an example of what you are aspiring to. Notice (and write down) how it makes you feel, what you admire about its craft, its voice, its use of language and imagery, the trajectory of its narrative. Let that experience set the tenor for your own writing session.
- **MEDITATE.** Choose a line or a word from a book, magazine, or love letter and meditate on it for ten minutes before writing.
- **BUILD IN "WASTED TIME."** Take ten minutes to e-mail, read your favorite blogs, or pet your cat before you start writing. Get the ants out of your pants right out of the gate so you can settle in.
- **GET BOTH SIDES OF YOUR BRAIN ON BOARD.** Handwrite questions for yourself about today's writing project with your dominant hand; answer them with your non-dominant hand.
- **EMPTY YOUR MIND.** Spend ten minutes writing with a specific goal being to purge your thoughts by committing them to paper.

Write out your worries, fears, plans, petty grievances. You're not trying to be literary here—your goal is to write those mental suitcases that are occupying your mind share into the overhead compartments where they can wait comfortably until your writing session is over. This is not only a really useful way to ground yourself for a productive writing session, it also may bleed some interesting themes into whatever comes next.

- **HAVE FUN.** Whether it's morning pages, a blog post, or a thank-you note, get that hand moving with something you enjoy that will wake you up and bring you back to your love of the word, your trust in your capacity, and your friendly feeling toward the page that lies in front of you, waiting to be known.

EXITING THE ZONE

Being conscious of how we complete our writing session is as important as the way we get started. Because if we feel good about what we accomplished and how we shifted gears from the writing trance back to the facts of our lives, we are far more likely to want to sit down to write again soon, and we are far more likely to feel successful when we do.

- **SET A CLEAR END TIME; STOP WHEN YOU SAID YOU WOULD.** Be reliable to your commitments to yourself, and you'll be willing to show up and do the work.
- **APPRECIATE YOURSELF.** Find at least one thing to celebrate about what you've accomplished or discovered during your writing time. Tell someone about it, or record it somewhere for yourself.
- **PUT OUT THE PILOT LIGHT.** Make sure you have at least an hour (ideally two) between writing and sleeping for the night so your writing pilot light can go out completely.

- **MAKE A CLEAR TRANSITION FROM YOUR WRITING SPACE.** Try doing some ritual of closure that is appropriate for where/how you write: Close the notebook, shut down the computer, close the door, change your clothes, whatever action says to yourself that you're finished for now.

- **SHIFT YOUR CONSCIOUSNESS.** Do a task or choose entertainment designed to take your mind to a different state. (My current mind-altering substance is the TV show *30 Rock*.)

- **CLEAN UP YOUR WRITING SPACE.** Put papers and files in order, bring the sticky coffee cups to the kitchen, and set the stage for your next successful session—so you'll want to sit down again soon.

- **LEAVE A TRAIL OF CRUMBS.** Close out your writing time with a line that is deliberately unfinished or specifically set as the starting place for the next time—so you'll have something to immediately pick up and run with when you return to your writing.

- **SET INTENTIONS.** Write a few notes about what you intend to do next with the piece you're working on. For example, call out what you know will need editing. Indicate where you'd like to reenter with some new first-draft writing. Bracket and checkmark what's working great. Indicate any questions or unresolved issues that you're still simmering on, with arrows to where the answers might land. Think of this as leaving the "future you" clues about what the "present you" already knows, so she will have the benefit of meaningful landmarks the next time this piece is entered.

- **SCHEDULE YOUR NEXT SESSION.** Making a commitment to yourself about when you'll be writing again before you completely close out each writing session can help maintain your momentum. Set a date and clear time parameters, such as: I intend to write next on Monday from 7:00 to 9:00 P.M. This way, even if you have to wait longer than you'd like, you have something specific to look forward to. And if you're resisting when the time comes, you have a specific promise to yourself to help keep you accountable.

- **BE GRATEFUL.** It's so easy to focus on our timing limitations. But I propose that you do the reverse. When you're wrapping up a writing session, whether it was five minutes in line at the post office or five hours at your desk, be grateful to yourself for finding the time, showing up, and making it happen. No one but you can keep your writing life moving forward. And you're doing it, one sitting (or standing) at a time.

RETURNING TO WRITING IN THE WORKS

> *When I've taken a long 'vacation' from a piece of writing, it's easy to return to it in overwhelm—to fall into a sea of fixes that are all crying out for my attention. To avoid this ceiling-caving-in feeling, I hone in on whatever passage/scene/chapter calls to me louder than the others. I refute my need to be chronological and start at the beginning of the piece. Instead, I wade right into the thick of what speaks to me. Every time, I find this technique leads me back into the piece in a much easier way."*
>
> —JORDAN E. ROSENFELD, *author of* Make a Scene: Crafting a Powerful Story One Scene at a Time

So what happens when you sit down to pick up where you left off and you balk? How do you ease yourself back into the spirit and momentum of your masterpiece? If your own tried-and-true techniques aren't working, or you don't yet have an effective strategy, try these:

- **TAKE IT ALL IN.** Sit down to simply enjoy what you've already written—without a pen in hand. Just let yourself appreciate what you've accomplished to date.

- **FOLLOW THE CRUMBS AND PICK UP THE THREAD.** If you've signed out of previous writing sessions as suggested in the Exiting the Zone section on pages 95 to 97, you are likely to have a line to lead into your latest writing session and some notes about what you believe needs work next.

- **MAKE A QUICK INVENTORY OF TODAY'S OBJECTIVES.** Time is the best editor. Having some distance from a piece in the works is the best possible way to know what to do with it next. Read your piece with your editor's hat on and take some quick notes about the revisions you intend to make.

- **DO WHAT'S EASY FIRST.** This is the most critical step. You don't want to scare yourself off by tackling what's hardest and giving up before you even get going. Instead, take a quick inventory of what needs doing and dive into whatever seems easiest—whether it's generating a new scene, coming up with a more powerful image, or fine-tuning dialogue. With a success or two under your belt, it will be far easier to approach the more complex challenges.

- **NOTICE WHAT WORKED AND REPEAT.** As you return to longer pieces over time, you'll develop your own systems for keeping your head in the game. Make note of what is working for you when you return to the page, and use those strategies as long as they are serving your writing.

FROM WORK AT YOUR JOB TO WORK AT YOUR DESK

For a few years in my twenties, my friends and I met every weekend to share the sculptures, sonnets, and songs we'd created. Over time, many of us changed our lives to enable us to make creative expression a top priority.

One day, a member of our group announced amazing news.

'I've saved up some cash,' he said. 'I just quit my day job. I'm going to write full-time!'

Forty extra hours a week? To write? I was incredibly envious. (Happy for him, but envious.)

My newly full-time artist friend did some good creative work at first, but as the months passed by, he got depressed. Without a daily structure and routine, he just couldn't focus.

He stopped making art."

—MARLA BECK, *poet and writing coach*

This is a good example of the dangers of leaping unprepared into the unknown. I think anyone who makes an abrupt transition from one way of life to another without careful planning can expect to be depressed and stymied—at least for a while. Routine and structure get built over time, and they are up to us to create. If you are in the habit of working within the structure that a job provides for you, and you leave that job to spend more time writing, it's going to take some very conscious and careful work to reinvent a rhythm that works for you.

- **EXPECT TO FLOUNDER AT FIRST.** Plan to "waste" at least a month as you settle into your new reality and find a new rhythm. No big deal. You probably have a lot of steam to blow off from that last job; let yourself have whatever you need to shake out the old and settle into the new.
- **WORK EFFECTIVELY AND EFFICIENTLY.** Establish a work space that sets you up for success (see chapter fourteen, page 138 for ideas).
- **BORROW STRUCTURE.** Make a list of what worked for you in the structure of your day job and start experimenting with implementing those structures in your own workday. For instance, you might set a finite start time, consider a standard work wardrobe,

establish a "commute," identify a set of colleagues, and create rules about accountability. Such rituals and boundaries may translate well to life as your own boss if you make them your own and hold yourself to them.

- **CREATE A REPORTING RELATIONSHIP.** Whether or not you appreciated your boss at your job, the fact is that being responsible for reporting results to someone else can keep us motivated and moving forward. Now that you are your own boss, you may want to involve someone else in your accountability to yourself. Communicate your chosen structure for your new writing life to a friend who has agreed to fill this role. At the end of each day or week, send that friend an e-mail with a brief recap of how you met your goals and expectations that day.

- **CELEBRATE SUCCESS.** This may sound like no big deal, but it is actually critical to your long-term results. It's easy to focus on what's not working in any given moment and put all your attention to struggling upstream. When you pay attention to and celebrate what is working as you establish your own writing career, you will be fueled not by struggle but by gratitude. In my experience, this trajectory is the most direct route between any goal and result.

Remember that your writing life is like your writing craft. It takes time to find its authentic voice and its true trajectory. Be patient with yourself as you navigate the transitions. Those in-between places are the trickiest, and they are full of potential.

THE MATH IS MAGICAL: YOU CAN PILE UP LOTS OF failures and still keep rolling, but you only need one juicy success to build a career.

The killer is the category called 'neither.' If you spend your days avoiding failure by doing not much worth criticizing, you'll never have a shot at success. Avoiding the thing that's easy to survive keeps you from encountering the very thing you're after.

And yet we market and work and connect and create as if just one failure might be the end of us."

—SETH GODIN, *best-selling author, entrepreneur, agent of change*

The Productive Writer transforms fear to faith by:

- Taking back the reigns from our inner critic.
- Accepting ourselves as we are today.
- Committing to taking risks and evolving along the way.
- Using fear as fuel.
- Respecting the wisdom of fear.
- Talking ourselves down from the ledge.
- Earning our stripes as fear veterans.

Fear is just a part of life—a useful part. It lets us know when there is danger. It lets us know when we are vulnerable. It advises us when to proceed with caution in unfamiliar territory.

But there are also instances when fear fails to protect us, and actually limits us. When we have an opportunity to grow (one that is not life threatening, of course) and don't take it because we are afraid, this creates more real estate for fear to move deeper into our psyche. So, in essence, the more we avoid fear, the more fear we create.

In contrast, when you walk toward what you fear in your writing life, you gain a sense of command of your destiny. Not only will you begin to trust that you can count on yourself to show up for the hard stuff, but you also learn the most valuable lesson of all: You will survive messing up, looking bad, and being rejected, and you will be far stronger for it. This kind of authority over your own destiny will serve you and your writing life well. I promise.

TAKING BACK THE REIGNS

Here's my theory. Fear is the unconscious belief that we are not good enough. It is the subliminal act of rejecting ourselves before anyone else has a chance to weigh in one way or another. Fear says, "You can't, you won't, so why even bother?" And I believe that fear is relational: We position ourselves as inferior to something or someone—usually imagined or wildly exaggerated. And compared to this "other" we don't measure up in our own eyes.

Who, exactly is holding this measuring stick? (We are.) Why do we give our power away like this to our inner meanie? (Habit.) Working with fear is a matter of taking your power back, to stop preempting yourself before you even figure out where your wings are and what their machinery might be. You can break this cycle right now.

Think Like a Dog

When I am working with my own fear, I refer to my dog Henry, who looks like a dwarf Lab, a thick, black bullet of a midsized dog on basset hound–sized legs. Due to his unusual proportions, he faces some unique ambulatory challenges. But Henry wrestles and fetches and begs with just as much passion and delight as the next dog. He doesn't seem bogged down with the burden of comparison—whether or not his normally proportioned canine sister performs better or worse than he does, for example. Rather, Henry focuses exclusively on what he wants and how to get it.

In my writing life, I try to think like Henry. I dive in because it's joyful to do so. I stay focused on the end goal without self-consciousness. And I don't worry about what anyone else is doing or how it might compare to how I'm doing—unless I see a strategy that's working well at serving up treats—those are worthy of cataloging and imitating.

Fear is just a feeling. You will survive it. And be stronger for it. It may even make you perform better. I promise.

FEAR AS FUEL

I've been performing publicly since elementary school and reading my writing to live audiences since my early twenties, and I'm often still terrified when I get up in front of a group of people. Every now and then, I'm fairly certain that I will pass out before I speak my first sentence.

But because I have made a choice to be terrified and do it anyway—hundreds of times, now—I have improved. A lot. And what I have learned is that fear can be an edgy, valuable source of fuel. It offers a huge adrenaline push that typically helps me perform far better

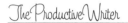

than I would in a less agitated state. Within a minute or two of standing in front of an audience, powered by fear, I generally land, connect with something authentic in me, and send that out to listeners. Then I start to relax.

Knowing you'll be afraid and trusting that you'll survive, and most likely even be successful, is a lesson that can only be learned the hard way: by doing what you fear and coming out the other side.

YOU ARE EXPERT ENOUGH TO TRY

I am a recovering perfectionist. My lifelong litany has been that I don't know enough, am not talented enough or impressive enough to present myself as an expert on anything, ever. This kept me from doing much of anything with my writing life for years. Then I had a rather simple but significant "aha" moment. I started noticing that writers who didn't seem to be any more perfect than I was were enjoying success.

It occurred to me then that maybe it wasn't my job to decide whether or not I was good enough. Instead, I decided it was my job to write to the best of my ability, take the risk of sending it out for publication, and let the folks who make such decisions decide whether my stuff was any good. This entirely revolutionized my writing life.

I want to be clear that I did not stop that inner voice from judging me harshly. I simply decided to step aside and focus on something else. I opened up the question of the worthiness of my writing to a wider audience, taking the chance that someone, somewhere might not be as negative as my own inner editor. And I was right.

The fact of the matter is this: While you're busy obsessing about not knowing enough about a particular topic or market (and therefore not taking the appropriate steps toward developing your expertise, understanding your market, and sending it out), some other writer is going to write down what he knows on that very topic and pitch it. This person is 100 percent more likely than you are to land the assignment, because he took the biggest step of all: Asking for it.

I'm not saying that you are guaranteed success in the form of publication, but you are guaranteed success in the form of evolution. Each
time you set a goal and move toward it, you learn. And you are expert
enough to do that right now. When you commit to listening to feedback, learning from rejection, and continuously refining your writing
and publishing skills, you will be doing everything you can to increase
the odds of getting the results you want.

So why not bury perfection's handcuffs in the backyard and get
down to the work of believing in what you are doing, trusting that
you will get better along the way, sending that query (or poem or short
story), and making the most of whatever comes next?

Rejection Is a Fact of the Writing Life—Even for Stephen King

Did you know that Stephen King was reportedly rejected forty-one
times before his first manuscript was accepted? Every writer who sub-
mits work for publication gets rejected. The majority of us get rejected
many, many, many times. In fact, the more published work a writer has,
the fatter his rejection file is likely to be. It's just the way this writing
business works. You could let fear stop you from submitting. Or you
could do whatever you need to do to prepare yourself for the inevitabili-
ties of rejection, and count every rejection letter as a badge of honor for
having the courage to try and for moving toward what you want.

One way to create some emotional distance is to pretend you're
sending out the work of someone you admire, instead of your own.
Early in my career, I would pretend I was submitting a colleague's
writing, someone I believed to be really fabulous and talented. This
made it easier for me to detach from the fear of what might happen
next. When the rejections came, I would hold them with compassion
as I would for that friend, which was far simpler for me to manage
than taking it all personally.

Another useful practice I've adopted per Natalie Goldberg's rec-
ommendation is to always have the next envelope stuffed, addressed,

and ready to go so the machinery of my submissions system is not interrupted by whatever emotions come up along the way. You may also be served well by looking to rejection letters as free editorial feedback that could help you make your work more polished and publication ready. And one last invitation: As that rejections file expands over the years, congratulate yourself for sending out so much work and for the faith in your own capacity that you have sustained along the way.

The most important thing to remember is that failure is frequently a stop along the way to the destination of success. Don't let fear derail you.

Try Another Way

When we set our sights on a goal and don't succeed, it's easy to tell ourselves a story that keeps us chained to this so-called failure. "I'm not [fill in the blanks with your own favorite insult here] enough to accomplish that," we may tell ourselves, then beat ourselves up with that story over and over and over, ensuring that we'll never try again. But it is just as easy to tell ourselves a different story when we didn't get what we wanted. And that story goes like this: "Well, that way didn't lead me to what I want. I will try another way."

These two sentences can be repeated for the next two days or two decades, however long it takes to find your way, that is, the way that takes you where you want to go. With this approach, there is no end point where we know for sure we can't and won't succeed. Instead, there is a spirit of practice and lighthearted fun. We are practicing getting somewhere and being creative about the ways and means of doing so. We are committed to the journey, and we are willing to keep moving in the direction we're headed, no matter what. With this kind of spirit and fortitude, eventually we get there—with a smile on our face and the humility to enjoy and appreciate our results.

Your job is not to be perfect. Your job is to find your way. Keep a log of what worked, what didn't, and what you intend to try next, and you'll always be moving toward where you want to go.

YOU'RE ALREADY DOING IT

I always wanted to be a creative writer but was never brave enough to really do it. The cost of failure seemed too great. So I pursued a number of other things—photography, art history, Asian studies. At some point in my mid-twenties, I quit my job in art history and found a writing job. One where I had to write a lot of articles, success stories, interviews—silly corporate things. But they gave me a lot of confidence that I could put sentences down on paper. Be persuasive. Provide information and direction. Frame things in a point of view. And I got comfortable doing that, and even a little confident. In looking back, this 'silly' writing job laid a great foundation for me as a more creative writer and more recently a poet."

—HEIDI SCHULMAN GREENWALD,
award-winning poet

How much do you want to bet that you're already doing whatever you're telling yourself that you don't know how to do and could never do in a million years? Maybe you're terrified of reading in front of an audience, but you just led a conference call at work. Maybe you are too scared to approach a short story, but you regularly make up bedtime stories for your child. When we don't allow ourselves to attempt what we really want head-on, often we come at it sideways, or crawl in the doggie door.

What small space are you shuffling around in that is echoing a larger playing field of your passion? Chances are good that the seed of your skill in this area has already been planted, and even watered, on the sly. Imagine what would happen if you simply brought it out into the light!

YES, THAT SUCCESS COUNTS

I often find myself arguing with students and friends who have a whole litany of reasons why their various successes "don't count." These folks always have a persuasive story about how they could have done better—published in a more reputable magazine or presented to a more prestigious crowd. Of course, there are always opportunities to do better. And in my experience, the most efficient way to approach those opportunities is by being grateful for what we are accomplishing right now. And understanding that we build slowly over time toward achieving our big goals with one tangible foothold at a time.

The truth is that no matter what your level of expertise and experience may be, chances are there's someone out there that knows more than you and someone who knows less. And no matter where your writing life takes you, this will always be true.

So why not just relax, put that notch in your belt, a clip in your scrapbook file, a link in your blog, or whatever you need to do to celebrate each and every opportunity and honor that comes your way? Don't berate the people admiring you (or berate yourself) if your current audience is not the Pulitzer Prize committee. We all have to start somewhere. I propose that you start by giving yourself permission to appreciate the success you have created, no matter how insignificant you might believe it to be. Right now. I know you can.

RESPECT THE WISDOM OF FEAR

When I was in elementary school, we celebrated dental health week with a cheery dental hygienist who joined our class and expounded on the basics of caring for our teeth. The grand finale of this visit (and my favorite part) involved chewing pink tablets, which would leave a pink residue in the places with plaque that needed more brushing.

I think of fear as the psychic pink residue that can bring our attention to the places that need care in us, if we let it.

Let's say you've tried working with fear using some of the approaches suggested in this chapter and that voice in you screaming wolf just isn't quieting down. No problem. This suggests that fear is imploring you, "tread tenderly here." You can do that. But first, you need to know more. So let's invite fear to tea and see what's on its mind.

Rewriting Your Relationship With Fear: A Dialogue With Yourself

Renegotiating your relationship with fear starts with hearing fear out, following it to its logical worst-case-scenario conclusion, and seeing what's possible from there. In my own writing life, I call this "talking myself down from the ledge." Here's an example:

I ASK	I ANSWER
What is my fear trying to protect me from?	Looking as dumb as I sometimes feel.
What is the worst that could happen if that outcome actually happened?	I would look as dumb as I feel; I would be publicly humiliated.
Could you get over this? If so, how long would it take?	Yes, I would get over it most likely in a week; at most, probably a month. (Plus, there are a lot of people in this world, and not everyone in the entire world will know how stupid I was. I could move somewhere no one knows me!)
Good; so it didn't kill you, even in your worst-case scenario, did it?	No. (But I'm still considering moving.)
What messages from family, teachers, editors, classmates, and/or colleagues are tied to this fear?	I have this sense that I'm not allowed to make mistakes; that perfection is the only acceptable option at all times. I think it was reinforced in various learning environments throughout my life, but most significantly by me.

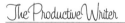

Do I believe in these messages and want to continue to invest in them?	Hell, no!
If not, what do I choose to believe instead?	I choose to believe that I will do the very best that I can, and that is all I can expect of myself. Perfection is not achievable, and mistakes are an inevitable part of learning. Looking dumb and feeling humiliated are well worth the discomfort of evolution.
What old stories and beliefs need to be retired to make way for success?	I need to practice untangling my worth from my accomplishments. This would make taking risks less scary and more fun. It would also take the charge out of making mistakes.
How will I manage my discomfort as I change my relationship with these patterns and start deprogramming fear from my nervous system?	I will take it slowly so I can notice the feelings that come up, write about them, and discuss them with my husband. I will ask for support when I need it. Most importantly, I will be willing to be uncomfortable. I know from experience that this discomfort won't last long, and that on the other side is greater confidence and ease (as well as many more mistakes).

WD Now, use the fear dialogue template at WritersDigest.com/article/productive-writer-downloads to see if there's a way to write yourself someplace new in relationship to your own fears.

You may be surprised at how much more authority you have over fear than it has over you.

EARNING YOUR STRIPES AS A FEAR VETERAN

I want you to keep a record of every little terrifying moment in your writing life where you transformed fear to courage. It will look something like this:

My Fear Journal

FEAR FACED	Speaking in public.	Submitting to journals I admire most.	Not capable of writing a book.
STORY FEEDING THE FEAR	I don't have anything worthwhile to say or the skills with which to say it.	I'm not yet good enough to be published in the magazines I admire most.	Generally not capable of doing anything I truly want.
ACTION TAKEN	Lectured at the Willamette Writers monthly meeting.	Sent an essay to *The Sun*.	Wrote the book.
NEW STORY, RELEASED FROM FEAR	I speak well in front of an audience; listeners seem engaged and interested, and I feel energized and excited once I'm up there.	I believe my work is on par with this publication's quality; there is no reason not to submit it there. If I am not accepted, I will submit to the next publication on my list, and the next, until it finds a home.	If I decide to do it, chances are that I can—even something really big and difficult. I will not likely believe it's possible until I've done it, and that's okay; as long as I stick with it and don't give up.

Download a template for your fear journal at
WritersDigest.com/article/productive-writer-downloads.com.

With this written record, over time you'll see (and start to believe in) your capacity to show up for yourself, no matter what your fear chats about in the background. In this way, one success at a time, you will enter into the realm of the alchemical where we write the straw of our fear into the gold of our faith.

Chapter 12

WRITING IN THE MARGINS OF A FULL-TIME LIFE

THE PRODUCTIVE WRITER CREATES A WORK-FAMILY-WRITING balance by:

- Appreciating the day job as an opportunity to develop a writing life.
- Making good use of daily commutes.
- Honoring both family time and writing time with her full attention.
- Getting buy-in from the family.
- Learning to say no (and yes).
- Lowering expectations.

We're all writing in the margins of a full-time life, regardless of what we do for money, when we sleep, who we live with, and what we expect from our writing. Writers today are busy. We have commitments coming out our ears. It is not easy to have children or partners or animals or jobs, and to write. Someone needs something much of the time. And yet, the writing must go on in a context that nourishes your health, happiness, and relationships.

IT'S ALL YOUR WRITING LIFE

It's easy to get frustrated that we're doing work or giving service that is perceived to be "taking away from our writing life" in some way. I don't choose to look at it this way, and I recommend that you don't either. The truth is that every single part of your life is your writing life. When you're changing a diaper, this is the writing life. When you are steaming the foam for a customer's latte, this is your writing life. When you are paying bills, driving carpool, setting the alarm clock to a cruelly early hour, this is your writing life.

This may sound as unromantic as tying your shoes, but the fact is that writing is just another thing that we writers do. And everything including the water cooler at work and the recycling bin in your driveway is a part of it. Even when you don't have time to write. Even when no one understands or praises or validates this dimension of your life. It's who you are, and you know it. That's all that counts. So, stop fighting the current of your life and struggling to be somewhere else. You are exactly where you need to be. This is your writing life. There is no other like it.

Of course, we always have the option of changing the reference points of our life. (For example, if you don't like the water cooler, go stand by the window. Chapter one offers a range of tips for reconsidering and reinventing life-work-writing possibilities.) But beware the temptation to get lost in the fantasies of what could be in that "ideal writing life" at the expense of perceiving what is possible right now. This chapter will equip you to work with everything you've got right this minute, so you don't waste one valuable drop of life energy that could be spent writing.

HONOR THY DAY JOB

Okay, so you don't love your day job. That's no reason to let it get in the way of your writing life. In fact, dissatisfaction with what you do for money makes it even *more* important to appreciate how the job funds what you *do* love: writing. I propose that you give props to that day job by making it as aligned with and attuned to your inner life as possible.

Tune In Instead of Tuning Out

Anna Sam was a grocery clerk in France. She didn't particularly like this job, which was supposed to be a stopgap between school and "adult life," but went on for a number of years. Rather than go numb to the disrespectful customers and various un-pleasantries of cashiering, she tuned into the trivial details of her uninspiring day job and went on to write the hugely popular *Tribulations of a Cashier*.

What are you avoiding at work that could actually serve your writing? How can you let irritation drive your imagination? Is there a way to work your professional learning curve—the humiliations and the triumphs—into a character's trajectory? Think of yourself as an archeologist and record interesting conflicts, surprising snippets of dialogue, industry jargon, and odd e-mails. Fueled with the energy and details of your days, your writing is likely to become more vital, and those hours spent working have the potential to become far more interesting as you mine them for insight and narrative.

Appreciate the Skills and the Character You Are Cultivating at Work

Are you better at meeting deadlines, collaborating with colleagues, solving problems, getting dressed and out the door at ungodly hours, or selling stuff thanks to your job? What character or career-building skills are you growing day by day that you can be proud of, invested in, and consciously developing in service to your writing? Make a list of the skills you are developing at your day job. Identify and appreciate how each one relates to and benefits your writing life. Refer to it any time you're feeling discouraged about "wasting time" at work.

For example, after writing and executing hundreds of marketing campaigns for clients over the years, I had a pretty good idea how to write the "Promotion" section of my first book proposal—and then follow through on those promises. I make a point of acknowledging this to myself, because it reminds me that what I do for my clients I am also doing for myself. Each skill I acquire in service to someone else's goals becomes a part of my own toolbox.

USE YOUR COMMUTE

If there's any way to take public transportation to work, take it. Use that time to read, write, and pay attention to the people and scenery around you. Let the rhythm, noise, and social stimulus of being jumbled together with strangers on a moving vehicle settle your noisy mind and awaken your sleeping senses. Have a notebook or computer easily accessible. Let your mind wander. Settle into the uselessness of in-between time and breathe in what is waiting for you there.

Stuck in the car? Listen to something on tape or CD that inspires or educates you. Keep paper and pen (or an audio recording device) close at hand for when you're stopped at lights or in traffic, and brainstorm ideas for your next writing project, or how to conclude that essay that just won't finish. Instead of letting the drive to and from work deplete you, use it to fill yourself up with ideas and language. Enjoy the opportunity to commune with yourself in that time and space when you are in between the demands of home and work.

Make the Rest of Your Life too Exciting to Resist

Bored and miserable out of your mind at work? Not a single one of these tips can make it any better? Okay. Then it's time for the I-hate-my-job challenge. I double dare you: Let this ill-suited employment propel you to make every moment outside of the day job as interesting, engaging, and writing worthy as it can be.

Julie Powell had a dead-end secretarial job and despondent lack of direction. To take the reigns of her life, she created her own personal adventure and writing challenge: cooking all 524 recipes in Julia Child's

Mastering the Art of French Cooking, Volume I, in a period of 365 days, and blogging about her experience. The blog took off, eventually to source the wildly popular *Julie and Julia: My Year of Cooking Dangerously,* first a widely read memoir and now a major motion picture.

How might you write yourself up by the bootstraps through a writing project that reminds you of (or helps you discover) who you are and where you're headed?

LOVE THE ONE YOU'RE WITH

Repeat after me: *When it's family time, it's family time. When it's writing time, it's writing time.* Period. The more completely you show up for each part of your life, the fresher you'll be when it's time to switch gears. In contrast, if you spend the afternoon playing with your kids stressing out about the deadline that needs to be met that evening, or you skip the important junior high ball game to meet the deadline but worry the whole time about not being there, you're revving (and exhausting) your mental and emotional engine unnecessarily. By the time you actually have the space to put your writing in drive, your emotional and physical gas tanks are likely to be dangerously low.

It took me a long time to learn this one, and I'm still learning it. When you keep your mind in the present tense—singing Old MacDonald to your child on the morning dog walk while galloping like a horsie with him on your back—rather than sending it (said mind) off on image-finding missions that leave you distracted and on the periphery of where you actually are and who you are actually with, you'll have far better relationships, both with the people and the writing in your life.

MAKE WRITING YOUR BABY

My friend and colleague Mary Thomas had two young children when I was just starting my own business. Her office hours were set to give her certain hours and days off of work when she was exclusively with her little ones. These nonworking times were nonnegotiable. Her children needed her, and that was that. Inspired by Mary's work/life structure, I have always tried to hold my creative writing life in this same regard: as dependent on me as a child, as high a priority. In this way, I have trained myself to honor the limits I set to protect my creative writing life. I encourage you to think about what you hold sacred and to put your writing life in that vessel, real or imagined, to protect it from any bad habits and sloppy time management.

WAKE UP EARLIER

The poet William Stafford famously wrote in the early mornings. At some point, it is reported that his young daughter caught on that this was a quiet time to find her father alone. She started waking early to visit with him, and Stafford would stop writing to spend time with her. I heard him interviewed about this. The interviewer wanted to know how he managed to get anything done with this kind of disruption. Stafford replied with a serene smile, "I just wake up earlier."

You can blame your circumstance or you can find time for what matters to you. The choice is yours. And at the end of the long day that started earlier than you'd prefer and included the writing that you value, the sense of accomplishment will be yours, as well.

GET BUY-IN FROM YOUR FAMILY

We held a family meeting once I decided to take my writing to heart, and I laid down the rules. First, if my door was shut, nobody knock unless the house is on fire or they are bleeding profusely. Otherwise, they had to deal with issues themselves, and some nights that might include fixing dinner. I told them that my writing was as important as their school, their sports,

and their social lives. Looking back, if I had not been so ada-
mant about the rules, they would not have taken my writing
seriously. The respect I gave myself spilled over to them. I
learned to let the dirty clothes pile up and my family learned
to help out around the house so I could write."

—C. HOPE CLARK, *freelance writer and editor of*
FundsforWriters.com

Anything you are doing that limits your time with the people you love is something significant to be held with the highest respect and negotiated carefully. (And, of course, the limits you set in framing your availability will be highly variable depending on the age and the needs of the people you care for, as well as the number of other adults available to help you support those needs.)

When you include your family in your writing goals by helping them understand what you are doing and what it means to you, you are far likelier to get buy-in, as well as emotional and practical support. Plus, when the people who love you are also excited about your writing life, it can help make all of you much happier along the way. Ask for help with a smile on your face and express appreciation when you get it, and you'll be on your way to establishing a new paradigm for your writing and your family.

LEARN TO SAY NO

Managing the needs, demands, and expectations of friends, family, and colleagues while also prioritizing your own need to write is nothing short of warrior's work. And there is a special samurai sword that you will likely spend the rest of your life learning to wield. Composed of two letters, *N* and *O*, this sword is the dividing line of your own self-respect and self-neglect. It allows you to participate in your own life and the lives of others with a clarity of purpose and conscience. (Of course, first it helps to be clear about what you are saying yes to. And you can learn more about this in chapter one.)

The secret to knowing when to say NO is being clear about what you are saying YES to.

In chapters one and four, you defined your realm of YES: a certain path of priorities and end goals. And because you developed a meaningful system for prioritizing tasks and managing your workload in chapter seven, you now have useful references to help you measure how much time and energy you might have to take on more. When you are asked to take on something new, you can decide how to proceed by asking yourself these questions.

Opportunity Checklist: The No Filter

- Does this opportunity move me toward my writing dreams, goals, or plans?
- Is this personally or professionally important to me?
- Do I have the time to take this on now? And if not now, is there a time in the foreseeable future when I could do it?
- How will my choice influence my relationships?
- How will this opportunity impact my ability to rest, recreate, and enjoy myself?
- What else in my life might need to take a backseat while I do it?
- Do I really, really want to do it? (What does my gut say?)

The more practice you have, the better you'll get at learning what requests are in line with who you are and what you expect from yourself and your writing life, and which you simply can't take on.

The Art of Saying No

And when it's time to say no, you want to be prepared to do it kindly and effectively, without leaving anyone in the lurch, or leaving the door of possibility slightly ajar. A few years ago when I was pregnant, writing a book, newly married, and working a full-time job, I launched "Operation Just Say No," where I clarified my YES and NO priorities, and then acted on them accordingly. Having had a lifelong YES-leading-to-over-commitment problem, I knew if I didn't set some serious boundaries for myself, I was likely to implode. I even created a brief boilerplate "no thank you" message to use; it helped me manage any resistance I might create for myself.

If you want to be highly productive, it's time to start saying YES to what takes your writing life forward and developing a discriminating relationship with that great gatekeeper NO.

"Operation Just Say No" Crib Sheet (My Example)

I will say YES to:

- All appropriate Sage Communications (day job as a marketing communications writer) work, within a forty hours/week scope.
- All work related to revising, finishing, and promoting *Writing the Life Poetic*.
- All self-care, baby prep, financial planning, and family building.
- Fun, rest, wonder, and delight!

I will say NO to: EVERYTHING ELSE

Boilerplate NO Message:

I so appreciate your interest, and think your project is [describe what I think/feel about opportunity]. Right now, with a full-time job, a full-time book project, and a baby on the way, my plate is overflowing. I wish you all

---

the best with [name of project], and I hope we will have a chance to work together in the future!

I will get out of: [I had a list of eight volunteer commitments that I sadly let go of, with a detailed exit strategy and timeline for each one, designed to transition responsibly and reasonably to the next person in charge.]

I will maintain: [Everything on this list fit within my YES categories and clearly had to happen for either income, contractual obligation, or sanity.]

LOWER YOUR EXPECTATIONS

My friend Kristin Berger is a beautiful poet and essayist, and an extremely engaged mother of two young children. We met as members of the literary collective VoiceCatcher when my son was just a few months old. As we became friends, Kristin gifted me a tiny pocket-sized composition notebook with a lovely little note welcoming me to the low-expectation writing club, with clear instructions that writing down one word at a time, whenever a word popped up, was just fine.

These were the new rules of early motherhood, and I was being initiated by a pro. Kristin is a wise woman; she understands well the mysteries of the margin, that word by word we write ourselves where we are headed.

I am often laughed at when I propose lowering expectations as a productivity strategy, but when folks are done laughing, they find they're breathing a little easier and that expecting a little less of themselves makes the work ahead feel far friendlier. And this is our goal, isn't it? To feel friendly with the words that come and the words that have yet to come. To let them know they are welcome here.

Chapter 13

FOR MANY WRITERS, THE WORLD WIDE WEB DOUBLES AS our virtual playground, office park, shopping mall, muse fuse, research library, back office, and school of life. There is so much to do and see and learn in the great wealth of information and opportunity online that it can be absolutely overwhelming—presenting big challenges to (and big opportunities for) a writer's productivity. This chapter will equip you to use social media and other online technologies to grow your platform and boost your productivity, without blowing your circuits!

DRIVE PLATFORM AND PERFORMANCE WITH SOCIAL MEDIA

Social media are online tools and technologies that let you easily connect with other people and create, then cultivate, the communities that matter to you. Writers have all kinds of reactions to and feelings about "going public" (using social media), from confusion to overwhelmed to distaste to delight. Whatever your personal preferences, the fact of the matter is that unless you are the next J.D. Salinger, you are more than likely going to be the number one person responsible for making yourself visible as a writer and known for your platform expertise.

So I'd suggest that you at least attempt to make nice with social media, with a goal of using it strategically and efficiently, while having fun. Once you are contacted by someone in your network who wants to quote you, hire you, or learn something from you; once you are uplifted, informed, or triggered to take productive action after hearing from or about someone online, you may gain a whole new appreciation for the virtues of online community.

Which Tools to Use, When and Why

A productive relationship with social media doesn't happen overnight. Like the rest of your productive writing life, it takes root one day at a time as you learn about the online communities and platforms that suit you best, then become increasingly effective at using them to listen, learn, and get your message out. You may want to consider adding at least a few of these communication vehicles to your social media arsenal:

- **BLOGS: BE YOUR OWN PUBLISHER.** A blog is a simple-to-use website that lets you post new information quickly and easily, whenever you want. Anyone who's interested can visit at any time, or subscribe. Through the comments function, readers can respond to your posts and dialogue with you as well as other readers. You can even automatically import blog posts to your Facebook page.

- **FACEBOOK: GET BY WITH A LITTLE HELP FROM YOUR FRIENDS.** As I write this, Facebook (www.facebook.com) may be the most popular way that writers sustain community and have fun online. You can share inspiration, news, questions, ideas, updates about your life and work, and connect with people you care about all over the world. Use it to announce events, opportunities, and publications. Some writers use their general Facebook page for this; others create a fan page and/or a group page where people who want to know about their platform or book or project can sign up to do so. Remember that the more pages you have, the more time and energy you'll spend keeping up with them. I recommend starting simple with one personal page and expanding as you have the time and interest.

- **GOODREADS: SHARE YOUR LITERARY LOVE.** If you want a forum for giving and receiving book recommendations, GoodReads (www.goodreads.com) is for you. You can also use it to track what you're planning to read and what you've already read, form a book club, or collect favorite quotes.
- **LINKEDIN: GROW YOUR PROFESSIONAL COMMUNITY.** Linked In (www.linkedin.com) allows you to keep in touch with colleagues, stay abreast of news and trends, showcase your expertise, join groups relevant to your interests, announce and learn about new opportunities, endorse the work of others, and receive endorsements. If you do only one thing there, post your résumé and a compelling description of what you do, for whom, and how it benefits them (and make sure to keep it current). You never know who might be seeking what you offer.
- **NING: CREATE A COMMUNITY ON YOUR TOPIC.** The Ning (www.ning.com) social platform lets you create a community around any topic that matters to you—enabling dialogue around the clock with anyone and everyone who's interested. You can use it to generate groundswell for your platform topic, collaborate with colleagues, or establish meaningful relationships with like-minded people.
- **TWITTER: SHOUT IT OUT IN SOUND BYTES.** Twitter (www.twitter.com) allows you to share brief news, ideas, information, and links (in 140 characters or less) with everyone who has chosen to "follow" you. Plus, you can follow everyone offering wisdom you're seeking on the craft, publishing, and platform-related topics that are most relevant to you. I recommend that you use TweetDeck (www.tweetdeck.com) as your tweeting interface to get a wide-angle view of what matters to you and be more efficient with how you sort, view, and navigate the news of your community.

Please note that this is not a definitive list of what's available in the realm of social media, nor can I begin to predict where we're headed. From where I sit, these are the most popular platforms that will give you the greatest opportunities to connect with a like-minded community today.

If you're using one of these tools already, maybe it's time to try another. If you're already engaged with every social media forum that is relevant to you, this is your opportunity to take a step back and consider how you can be even more effective with the time you spend online. (More details about time management on page 128.)

Put Your Finger on the Virtual Pulse

In addition to putting the people you want to know at your fingertips, technology can be extremely useful in delivering the information you are seeking to your desktop, around the clock.

- **TRACK TOPICS AND TRENDS.** Google Alerts (www.google.com/alerts) is a great, free tool you can use to plug in your platform keywords and get a daily, aggregated list of articles and links where those words or phrases appear. This is a fast and simple way to keep your finger on the pulse of your chosen topic or area of expertise. I also recommend tracking your own name and book titles, so you can easily learn what's being said about you as soon as it happens.

- **ARCHIVE YOUR FAVORITE SITES.** Bookmark the websites you visit frequently. Then organize your list by creating a bookmarks toolbar and menu in your browser; you can even create these in Google so you can log into them from any computer you're using, anywhere.

- **SAVE TIME STAYING CURRENT.** Google Reader (www.google.com/reader) is a handy tool that lets you cull every blog and site you read regularly, sorted in folders by topic of interest, in one

fast and friendly interface. Often you'll even have the option to tweet about news that you want to share, directly from your Google Reader page. This can significantly streamline the time you spend learning and sharing information online.

Grow your system over time by filing each new Web resource within the appropriate menu library or Google Reader folder as you go. One day at a time, you'll be charting your own personal media constellation and making it easier and easier to navigate at the speed of light.

SETTING BOUNDARIES AND BEHAVIOR STANDARDS

If you were to partake in all that is available to you online, you wouldn't have much time left over for actually writing anything. Knowing what you value, what you expect, and what your limits are will help you stay on course so you are using social media to service your productivity, rather than letting it derail you with distraction.

Understand How Social Media Is Serving Your Productivity and Platform

Connect with people who share your interests or expertise

Today it doesn't matter where you live: If you are trying to quit your marshmallow sandwich habit, it's quite likely you can find people all around the world in exactly the same predicament, with all kinds of ideas and resources and encouragement to share. As you develop your platform and your craft, you have the opportunity to do so in good company at any time of day or night. Since you're likely to be at your computer while writing, these people you join forces with are often more accessible than many of the other people in your life. They're right there at your fingertips, accompanying you as you go.

Exchange support, encouragement, and opportunities

The good people in your online community are the ones who will likely want to interview you on their blogs, announce your good news, offer publication suggestions, and generally share, collaborate, cheer, and kvetch with you through the ups and the downs of your writing adventure—and vice versa. How does this happen? Through reading and commenting on blogs that appeal to you, participating in forums, joining groups related to your topic or genre, responding to tweets and Facebook posts that are aligned with your platform and passions, starting or joining a relevant Ning community, and so on.

Offer and tap wisdom

Having a presence online (through a blog, Facebook, Twitter, or other social media communities discussed in this chapter) gives you a pulpit, a bullhorn, a virtual rooftop from which to shout about all the good news and interesting insights you discover along the way. If you do this well and regularly, it is likely that people will start seeking you out for the wisdom you have to offer on your topic (as well as the unique spirit in which you share it). Over time, you will have the opportunity to establish yourself as a thought leader. Likewise, you can subscribe to have the insights and expertise of any number of thought leaders coming to you directly, every day.

Do it faster

If you could do it online faster and more efficiently, would you? Over the years, I've taught in a wide range of contexts, including universities, hospitals, conferences, libraries, and community centers. I love teaching live. But the realities in this chapter of my life are that I can connect with more people, more easily, right from my desk—without having to leave the house, get dressed, find childcare, or take time to travel. Plus, I get to learn with poets all over the world without schlepping a suitcase. Ask yourself if there are any advantages or efficiencies to taking whatever you're doing "live" online, whether it's teaching, research, interviews, or community events.

Get inspired

Social media offers a multitude of ways to study productive writers you admire. Learn where they're publishing, how they communicate with their community and their readers, what types of projects they're currently fielding, and how they sustain a momentum over time. Some talk frankly about where they're sending out work, what they're getting paid, why they think you should try harder in some areas and give up in others. Should you get intimidated along the way, remember that every great writer was at one time unknown and unpublished. Your opportunity here is to get inspired by what others have accomplished and to learn how you can apply the approaches you admire to take your own platform and productivity forward.

Most importantly, if you want to use social media, find what's fun, interesting, and surprising in it for you, so you'll keep on doing it. And evaluate along the way if and how it is serving your writing life.

Make a Social Media Game Plan

You'll get the most benefit from your relationship with social media if you know and respect your limits. Every writer's needs and requirements for social media will be unique, depending on temperament; available time; promotional, platform-development and community-building priorities; and the amount of pleasure it gives you.

When you are ready to take the reigns in your relationship with social media, spend at least a few weeks getting a sense of your current rhythms, tendencies, and habits. Notice what seems to be serving you well, where you waste time, and where you're getting the most value from the time you spend. Then create a social media game plan to set some standards for yourself.

Don't worry if your plan isn't perfect at first; know that you'll be refining it over time as you know more and more about what you want and need from your relationship with social media as your productivity and your platform evolve.

 Check out an example of a social media game plan at WritersDigest.com/article/productive-writer-downloads.

REIGNING YOURSELF IN

Okay, so you've set some online performance standards for yourself. Now it's time to enforce them.

Break the Link

While writing this book, our home computer network went down. Which meant that my laptop could no longer go online without physically plugging it in. I encouraged my husband—our family tech expert—not to fix it. And when the book woke me at 4:30 in the morning, as it did on most mornings, I'd stay in bed with the computer and write and write and write without having to manage my feverishly insistent desire to jump online. It simply wasn't an option. Cafés that require a payment to tap into their online network serve a similar purpose. I don't pay and enjoy a blessed writing session free of virtual noise. Sometimes the best way to enforce a boundary is to eliminate all choice. How can you break the link between you and things you do online to distract and interrupt your writing?

Drive Your Performance With Your Media Habit

Let's say you love Facebook. Set that up as your carrot to get you over a hurdle you've been circling instead of jumping. Give yourself a clear limit, and promise yourself a reward on the other side. For example, I will commit to two hours of writing, and then allow myself a look-see (with a time limit) online. The imagined reward keeps me in my seat and ensures that I'll delay gratification long enough to actually

accomplish something. What are you willing to wait for in the name of productivity?

Do What Moves You From Moment to Moment

The paradox of setting strict guidelines about how and what you're going to do online is that some days, it just won't work. Every now and then, the most productive thing you can do is surf the Web for an hour, or however long it takes, to ground yourself and get the wanderlust out of your system. If you force yourself to do what you're really not ready to do, sometimes that just leads to rebellion, and rebellion is not productive.

Letting yourself off the hook of structured expectation just may be the most direct route to actually accomplishing writing on the other side. Think of this option as your bathroom hall pass, and watch yourself carefully. If you're excusing yourself every few hours for days at a time, then it's time to tap into one of this book's other strategies to get your groove back.

Understand That Everything You Say Online Is "On the Record"

With the advent of social media, gone are the days of one-dimensional identities in the various compartments of our lives. In places like Facebook and Twitter, we are sharing who we are; maybe not all of who we are, but certainly more than was once typically communicated on the job or in each aspect of the many roles we play in life. We can see the old prom photos and latest family photos of the people we may have otherwise only seen in business suits. We learn that they tap dance and design greeting cards in addition to running a publishing house or editing that magazine we're dying to crack. We witness what's troubling them and what they're curious about.

A Productive Writer is clear about what types of information she is willing to share and how. Consider carefully that any complaint you make about anyone online will eventually reach them. Any "secret" thing you publish is just a link away from going viral. And any detail you reveal about your personal life that you wish you didn't will be retrievable to anyone and everyone forever after. So be extra careful about what you say online and the spirit in which you say it. Everything you express should be a reflection of the standard you set for yourself in your writing life. Be on your best behavior (unless you are growing a "bad behavior" platform, of course), be respectful, and understand that everything you say online will be on the record—forever.

LOOKING TO THE FUTURE

We writers are entering a brave, new publishing frontier full of many unknowns and possibilities. The proliferation of content delivery media is leveling the playing field and putting publishing and platform development opportunities in our hands like never before. As e-books (via Kindle and other such technologies), iPad applications, and the concept of content as product take root in the zeitgeist, we need to pay attention, listen, learn, and remain as nimble as we can. Why? So we can understand the opportunities as they approach, get a handle on the technologies and what they offer, and decide how to harness the appropriate ones in service to our productivity, visibility, and success.

Chapter 14

MASTERING YOUR MOMENTUM

> A PRODUCTIVE WRITER SUSTAINS MOMENTUM BY:
>
> - Starting where you are.
> - Claiming your carrot—finding the motivation that keeps you going.
> - Filling your cup with information and inspiration.
> - Creating a high-performance work space.
>
> Every writer works differently. The very same processes that keep you engaged with your creative process and achieving your desired results could stop another dead in her tracks. This chapter offers some big-picture principles, strategies, systems, and encouragement. It also invites you to become your own best creativity consultant and productivity coach. After all, who knows what you want, what you resist, and how you might bring these two into alignment better than you?
>
> ### START WHERE YOU ARE
> How does one grow into a productive writer from a wannabe writer? How do we train for the marathon of the writing life in a way that keeps our eye on the prize without losing appreciation for the ground under our feet right now? Here are a few ideas.

Just Get It Down

When you're riding a bike, you need a certain amount of forward momentum to stay upright. If you sit on the seat and don't turn the pedals, you're likely to tip right over. The writing life is the same way. In the first draft-writing stage, just being in motion and getting words down on the page is the most important part. The moving hand leads to more writing. A standstill of critical editing in this getting-it-down phase will send you right over the handlebars. I'm going to mix my metaphors here and encourage you to write as if you are laying down bricks, one after the other. None is more worthy than the next; each has its part to play as your writing takes shape. The composite will eventually add up to something whole. But you're not thinking about that just yet. For now, your job is to lay the words down as they arrive. Let them show you what kind of edifice wants to come through.

Ride the Wave

Feeling a part of something larger than my own personal word-creation silo usually helps me write more and enjoy the process more. The same might be true for you. If you'd like to spend a month wringing every drop of writing out of you—in the company of a huge community of others who are doing the same—you might want to participate in one of these two challenges:

- **NOVEMBER IS NATIONAL NOVEL WRITING MONTH** (NaNoWriMo), where hundreds of thousands of writers all over the world log in more than 1,000 words per day, with a goal of writing one 50,000-word novel from scratch in a month's time. (www.nanowrimo.org)

- **APRIL IS NATIONAL POETRY WRITING MONTH** (NaPoWriMo). A popular, somewhat recent tradition that happens in this month

is the poem-a-day challenge. Check out Robert Lee Brewer's blog, Poetic Asides, for a great daily prompt and a committed poetic community. (blog.writersdigest.com/poeticasides)

And if these opportunities to write in community don't sharpen your pencil, start your own tradition, invite a few friends to join you (and hold you accountable to the work and the fun), and then get going.

Practice Makes Perfect Possible

Every time you sit down to write, no matter what you're writing, how accomplished you believe yourself to be, or how high the stakes, think of what you're doing as *practice*. Why? Because it takes the pressure off and keeps humility front and center. Who needs the performance anxiety of striving for (the impossibility of) perfection? I sure don't, and I don't think you need it, either. Practice is a gentle way to hold ourselves accountable to high expectations with a loose and friendly grip on the reigns. The more we practice, the more possible our writing will become. And the more confident we will be in our ability to show up at the page and make something interesting happen there.

Impatience Killed the Writing

Curiosity may have killed the cat, but impatience is definitely the most lethal attitude for a writer. I have an essay I've been trying to finish since the mid-nineties. If I were attached to the reward of finishing rather than the reward of figuring, the pilot light of my engagement with this craft would have gone out long ago. The same is true with publishing. We all are ready to make our work visible to the world at different times, and we all have completely unique trajectories of how that happens. My poetry collection took shape over the course of fifteen years, and my first nonfiction book proposal was birthed through a hard, fast labor of one month, yet it encompassed a lifelong gestation of ideas and practice.

I propose that you think of your writing consciousness as a Crock-Pot that will be on a slow boil in the kitchen of your mind/body/soul for the rest of your life. It will nourish and sustain you if you are willing to feed it and let it feed you. Over time, you will add ingredients, become more subtle in your seasoning, and eventually start producing elaborate meals. In the meanwhile, you'll be far too busy laying down words on the page to watch the pot that has yet to come to a boil.

Stop Trying So Hard

One phenomenon happens so reliably for me that I propose it is a kind of natural law for writers. It goes something like this: The idea I am trying to capture or problem I am attempting to solve will inevitably sort itself out once I stop "working." I leave my desk to scoop the cat litter, and BAM: There is the answer, clear as a clump of clay. The fact that it's happened hundreds of times, however, has not made me more inclined to trust the process. I have a tendency to want to push things through to my own idea of what completion should be, and I am reminded again and again that things simply don't work that way, at least for me. It seems like a paradox: When we stop trying so hard, we meet less resistance from what we want to "fix."

Anyone who has experienced the difference between forcing a toddler into his car seat vs. motivating him with excitement about what a big boy he is, knows what I'm talking about. Sometimes, you just have to get your will out of the way, bring in that cheerleader who believes you can do it, and step aside. That little toddler in you knows just how to get around the obstacles you've presented him with—if only you will let him.

Be Willing to Not Know

Many writers don't know exactly where they're headed with a piece of writing, whether it is a 20-word poem or a 50,000-word nonfiction book. Even if they have a detailed outline or a very specific idea in mind of what their destination may be, and even if they arrive at said destination, the specific trajectory is likely to reveal itself along the way. You can expect to not know any number of things as you are writing—even the reason you are writing. You can trust that what wants to be known will make itself evident along the way. Your job is to be in motion, be willing to be surprised, and follow where you are led. (If this makes you nervous, don't worry. There will be plenty of time for steering, that is, editing, along the way. But try holding off on the known for as long as you can while you let the unknown have its way with you first.)

CLAIM YOUR CARROT

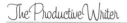

> 'Nobody cares if you write.' On the surface, it might sound discouraging, but this motto has actually helped me maintain a long career as a freelance writer. Sure, your agent and publisher care once you have a book deal. But in the early stages of crafting a novel or unassigned story, poem, or article, you're on your own. The trick is to figure out where your motivation lies. Find the enjoyment (or at the very least, the money!) in your work. And, yes, money can be a motivator. After all, as freelance writers we have bills to pay, and not everything we write is going to be fun and easy. The boring, steady work is what allows me time to write the fun, creative pieces that may or may not get published."
>
> —Wendy Burt-Thomas, *author of* The Writer's Digest Guide to Query Letters

Staying motivated with writing is as personal a process as choosing dessert (or a vegetable). That's why I'm going to invite you right now to name and claim the carrots-on-sticks that work best to keep you moving forward toward your goals. As Wendy Burt-Thomas has so eloquently explained, various dimensions of your writing life may be devoted to different carrots. The key is to be clear about why you're in motion, and to give yourself a mighty good reason to keep up the good work. In short, let the imagined reward drive the motivation.

Let's consider an example of a single writer's various types of work and how she might stay engaged with each one:

Motivation Master Plan

GOAL	MOTIVATION/REWARD
Write a poem	· Emotional release · Discovery · Delight · Share with a friend
Finish and publish "Tis the Season to Write Poetry" article	· Share wisdom · Earn money ($) · Gain visibility · Grow platform
Write, edit, and project manage ongoing corporate newsletter project	· Support family ($$$) · Fund time for creative writing · Keep writing chops and strategic thinking solid · Keep relationship-building and communication skills honed
Author nonfiction book about poetry	· Share wisdom and delight · Accomplish major writing goal · Grow platform · Expand possibilities for future teaching and information sharing · Earn money ($$) · Have fun

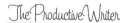

Teach poetry classes and workshops	• Get people excited about what is possible in poetry
	• Earn money ($$)
	• Have fun

As we discussed earlier in this chapter, maybe you don't yet know what your carrots are or why; that's ok. You can invent reasons and rewards as placeholders to get you out of the gate. And as you understand more about your process, you can revise your Motivation Master Plan as you go. What's most important is that you get moving and find a way to sustain the momentum. And the more you practice, the better you will know how to make this happen.

 Now create your own Motivation Master Plan! For a template visit WritersDigest.com/article/productive-writer-downloads.

CREATE A HIGH-PERFORMANCE WORKSPACE

Having a workspace that enables your effectiveness can make a big difference in sustaining a productive writing momentum. And the trick is to make the most of what you have, while striving for optimal conditions.

When I first started my marketing consulting business in my mid-twenties, my "office" was a small white desk I bought at a yard sale; it sat in the bedroom I shared with my boyfriend within the home we shared with another friend. Throughout the day, our roommate—who worked construction at irregular hours—would play electric guitar with his friends on the other side of our paper-thin bedroom wall where his bedroom happened to be. I'd try to time calls with clients to the times I'd be alone in the house, but this was nearly impossible to predict.

Needless to say, this wasn't the ideal professional setup, but it was good enough to get me going. And it was an important lesson in simultaneously holding an ideal vision for the future (my own private, quiet office) while making do with the real. We start where we are, and we work with what we've got. It was five years before I had an office to call my own. But progressively, with my eye on that prize, my circumstances and finances improved until I eventually achieved that goal; once I did, boy did I appreciate it.

With cell phones and laptops at our disposal today, we writers have many options for how and where we do the business of writing and communicating with the people we need to reach to make our writing and publishing happen. Following are a few suggestions for making the most of your workspace.

Ergonomics: Balance Comfort and Stimulation

You want to be comfortable as you work, but not so comfortable that you'll be tempted to take a nap. A chair with good back support (ideally one made for the office) and a keyboard at the right height for your hands to avoid excess strain are the most important elements. Decent lighting, attention to your posture, and regular stretching can give your body what it needs to perform well and your mind what it needs to sustain attention.

Communicate Impeccably

Writers need to communicate. And they need to do so easily and with some semblance of professional decorum. I recommend the following:

- **PHONE.** Either get a dedicated phone or figure out how to make the one you share behave like a dedicated professional line. The voice-mail greeting you record for callers can go a long way toward making it clear that this is the place to do business with you.
- **E-MAIL.** Many of the people you'll be collaborating with in your writing life—editors, publishers, agents, clients, interviewees—will be easiest to reach by e-mail. Make sure you use an e-mail

address that is professional, ideally has your name and website in it (sage@sagecohen.com; sage@sagesaidso.com), and is hosted by a reliable ISP. Also, don't miss the opportunity to use your e-mail signature (the few lines that you can format to appear at the end of every message) to share your contact information, promote upcoming events, announce publications, and share the good news of your writing life with others.

- **FAX.** While most documents travel by e-mail these days, you still may need a fax for occasions such as sending and receiving signed contracts. Earlier in my career when fax was a more common communication channel, I had a fax machine that shared a phone line. Today, I find it simpler and more cost-effective to use a service that sends me faxes received through my e-mail. When I need to send a fax, which is very infrequently, I drive to Kinko's (now Fed Ex Office) and do it there. I encourage you to figure out what is simplest and most cost-effective for you.

- **ONLINE ACCESS.** Operate at the speed of a Productive Writer. Ensure that your online connection is fast enough to keep up with the research, social media, e-mail, and other performance demands of your work. Plus, you'll need some solid strategies for managing your time online. (More about that in chapter thirteen.)

- **PRIVACY.** Whether you're conducting phone interviews or simply need to hear yourself think, privacy is an extremely important variable in the writing life. You may enjoy the "privacy" of sitting in a bustling café and doing your work there, when you don't need to be on the phone. Or you may need to sit in a hermetically sealed space where not a peep penetrates. If there's any way you can set things up so you're not distracted

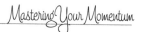

by the sounds around you when it's time to write, that is the ideal. I know a mother who takes five-minute writing breaks in the bathroom. Whatever your creative shrine or strategy may be, protect it as best you can with privacy.

Woo Your Computer

- **DON'T SKIMP ON COMPUTER CARE.** Treat your hardware and software like the good friends that they are. Use a computer whose performance is reliable and mechanics are sound.

- **DEFENSE IS THE BEST OFFENSE.** Get whatever virus protection is appropriate for your machine, and run the proper disk utilities at the recommended times to help keep your computer's processing as unmuddled as possible.

- **BACK UP, BACK UP, BACK UP!** I think this is so important that I do a double backup—one to a secondary hard drive on my desk and one to an off-site server. The last thing any writer needs to deal with is the loss of that vast archive of words sitting in the little box on our desk. Don't let it sink to the bottom of the ocean without a plan for retrieving the treasure. (More about this in chapter nine.)

- **USE PROGRAMS THAT SHOW YOU'RE A PROFESSIONAL.** Make sure you're using word processing and other programs that are up-to-date enough to easily exchange documents and other information in a professional manner.

Creating Boundaries to Protect Your Writing Time

Every Productive Writer has a completely unique context of how and where she writes. The best way to protect your writing time is to clearly articulate for yourself what your office hours are, and then communicate them clearly to the people who need to know.

Perhaps your business clients need to understand that you're in the office Tuesday through Thursday, 9:00 A.M. to 5:00 P.M., or your family needs to know what times you are not to be disturbed. Even if your office hours change regularly, my invitation to you is to establish a concrete system that lets you and everyone living and working with you know what to expect of your writing time. Then stick to it.

No Office? No Problem. Create an Office in a Box.

Let's say there is absolutely no corner of your living space that works as a permanent writing nook for you, and working in a public space is either undesirable or not possible. No problem. I recommend that you create an office in a box: a collection of key items that you want and need when it's time to set up shop to write. (Notebooks, laptop, a few pens and highlighters, file folders, sticky notes, and a nice-smelling candle might comprise a basic starter kit.) Once the kids have finally gone to sleep and the kitchen is quiet and clean, reinvent it as your work space. Take the office-in-a-box out of the pantry, set up at the kitchen table in two minutes, and go.

Create a Context of Abundance

I have an electric tea kettle in my office. It makes me feel like the queen of the universe to be nowhere near a kitchen, press a button, and have steaming water a minute or two later. I also light a yummy-smelling candle while I work; this has a feeling of spiritual ritual for me and helps me land in my work. It costs me maybe a few cents each time I light a candle or pour a cup of tea. And yet I feel like I am in the lap of luxury. How can you create a simple, affordable context of abundance in your writing ritual that sets you up for success?

Clear the Chaos

 You are disorganized if you need something somewhere that you don't have or have something somewhere that you don't need."

—DAVID ALLEN, *author of* Getting Things Done and Getting More Out of Life

Some writers work beautifully in chaos. If you're like me and need every surface everywhere around you to be ordered and serene before you can start writing, it's time to start investing in that reality. One day at a time, one drawer or folder at a time, tackle what stands between you and the results you want. Take five minutes while you're on the phone to sort, file, and purge a pile. Start each writing session with a small ritual of making order, using some of the skills and strategies recommended in chapter nine. Don't forget those closets crammed full of the stuff you don't want to look at. You'll be amazed at how clearing them will settle the background noise of your mind.

Remember how Goldilocks just kept on eating porridge and bouncing on beds because she couldn't get quite comfortable? Your writing life may feel a bit like a borrowed home for a while, too. But stay committed to stepping into your own momentum, and you're likely to find a productive writing rhythm that fits just right for you.

Chapter 15

FIRST DRAFTS

> *I ALWAYS DO FIRST DRAFTS OF MY POEMS ON YELLOW paper. Because yellow paper means it is just a draft, I am much braver and more wild than I would be on white paper. Those yellow-paper scribbles make me more free than I would be on the computer where everything looks like a final copy."*
>
> —PENELOPE SCAMBLY SCHOTT, *author of* A Is for Anne: Mistress Hutchinson Disturbs the Commonwealth *(Oregon Book Award for Poetry, 2008)*

The purpose of a first draft is to set your stake in the ground of uncharted territory, to prove to yourself that you know how to go there and to stay out of your own way long enough to let the words come in a way that feels natural, authentic, and fun. I like to think of my first drafts as very young children. They need a certain amount of freedom to move outside the rules in order to find their own footing and anchor their unique spirit. Simply put, first drafts are to be indulged and given whatever makes them happy. *No* may trigger a tantrum, and puddles were *made* for jumping in, silly. Here are a few other possibilities that may delight your first drafts and keep them zooming until nap time.

- **USE A SPECIAL FONT** for first drafts that feels friendly and fun. (I use Cambria for first drafts and Times New Roman for final.)

- **CHOOSE A COLOR PAPER** that makes you feel courageous, whether you're writing by hand or printing from your computer.

- **EXPERIMENT WITH INPUTS AND CONTEXT** such as location, music, lighting, time of day, writing medium (such as pen and paper vs. computer) to get yourself in the mood. Often, I'll start something in a café or in bed, two low-pressure environments where I feel relaxed and comfortable. My desk is a place steeped in a long history of "serious" work, and it can feel a little imposing to start there.

- **AIM LOW, CELEBRATE HIGH.** I spent ten minutes celebrating my toddler son today as he proudly placed the top on a plastic container and then pulled it off again. This is a significant developmental accomplishment for him, and the pride was evident on his face. You want to be this impressed with yourself as you work on your first draft. You want your attitude to be one of marveling at every single word that hits the page, and when the words run dry, tell yourself how much you appreciate yourself for getting as far as you have come. That's it. No judgment. No revisions. Just an admiring witness of all that you've done to make this first draft happen.

- **BUILD YOUR FRAME FIRST.** If you are writing an article or business communication that has a specific message you want to come through or thesis that needs to be proven, it can help to start by writing a high-level outline or even bullet list of the big-picture progression of ideas. If you roughly sketch out what you are positing, and the key points that will prove it, you'll have the undergirding in place and can simply add flesh to the bones.

Even if the structure changes along the way, which often it does, it's easier to pull out a doorframe when you have a sense of structure that is solid beneath you.

For more general suggestions about facing the blank page, check out chapter ten.

HOW AND WHEN TO REVISE

After you are absolutely sure that your first draft gas tank is completely empty, it's time to revise. How, when, and why you revise is going to be a very personal experience that you cultivate over time. But some big-picture guidelines may help give some structure to your process.

- **CHOOSE AN EDITING TOOL THAT FEELS FRIENDLY.** If I'm editing on the computer, I use the "track changes" feature in Word so I can easily see what I'm changing and have a record of what has been deleted. If there's a section that I know needs work but I don't have a specific editing idea for it yet, I'll highlight that in yellow so I can remember that it needs my attention. If I'm working on paper, I use a colored felt-tip marker—any color but red—because it's easy to see and doesn't give me that teacher-doesn't-approve feeling that red ink tends to conjure.

- **EDIT IN THREE PHASES, FROM MACRO TO MICRO.** Imagine that your editing eye is a camera panning in from a great distance.

    1. In the first round of revision, you want to stay up high and do a big-picture analysis of your piece, taking notes as you go. Where is it headed/what is it accomplishing? What is working well? What needs to be cut? What needs further development? How is it aligning (or not) with your objectives? Make any big-picture changes that don't

require fine detail. Once you have a good overview of where you're headed next, take a break from the piece.

2. Return rested and refreshed, preferably after a full day away. Round two is tactical. You zoom in to ground level where it's time to do the heavy lifting of rewriting, re-imagining, honing voice, dialogue, imagery, narrative arc, sound, strategic impact, and whatever is relevant to the objectives of your particular piece and the parameters of your craft. Until your eyes are crossing. Really.

3. Again, take some time and space from your writing, then prepare for some fine-tuned polishing. Make sure spelling, grammar, and verb tense alignment are in tip-top shape. Scrub every image to a shine; enliven dialogue with the most energetic verbs and adjectives; see how far you can cut back language to its most potent and relevant core.

4. (Bonus step) Repeat all of the above, in sequence, as necessary until you get that little satisfied plunk in your chest that tells you it's time to stop. (Or follow the steps on page 152 of this chapter for some more concrete guidelines toward finishing.)

Remember, there is no time limit to revising as a rule, unless of course you have a specific deadline you must meet. If you have the time to let a piece sit when you get stuck, that's my vote. In my experience, time is the best editor. When you return to an unfinished piece of writing with a little distance, chances are good that you'll have more useful insights than you did at your last sitting. I hope you will take it slow at first and really get a feel for your own editing rhythm. The more you practice, the more natural and confident you'll feel and the better your results will be.

, do recommend that you name and save your multiple versions ,ng a system that makes sense to you and is easy to find and retrieve. ɔee chapter nine for ideas about how to easily find the version you need, when you need it.

PRACTICE DELIBERATELY (AND HIT YOUR TARGET)

> *The best people in any field are those who devote the most hours to what the researchers call 'deliberate practice.' It's activity that's explicitly intended to improve performance, that reaches for objectives just beyond one's level of competence, provides feedback on results, and involves high levels of repetition.*
>
> *For example: Simply hitting a bucket of balls is not deliberate practice, which is why most golfers don't get better. Hitting an eight-iron three hundred times with a goal of leaving the ball within 20 feet of the pin 80 percent of the time, continually observing results and making appropriate adjustments, and doing that for hours every day—that's deliberate practice."*
>
> —GEOFFREY COLVIN, *senior editor-at-large,*
> Fortune Magazine

Have you ever gotten halfway through a piece of writing and found yourself floundering about what you were actually trying to accomplish in the first place? This is where the concept of deliberate practice comes in. When you set your sights on specific goals for a piece of writing, you'll know exactly how close you come to achieving your goal. Try writing out as many of these details at the top of your piece, or on a sticky note that you attach to your computer screen or your working file folder. For example, I wrote this at the top of a recent piece I'd been contracted to write:

- Target word count: 1,500
- To appear in: *Poet's Market 2011*
- Audience: Aspiring poets with varying levels of experience getting published
- Topic: Self-publishing—my path and process

I challenge you to name and claim the key objectives of every piece of writing, even a blog post, short story, essay, or poem, regardless of whether you've been hired to write it or if you ever intend to share it. Here are a few tips to get you started:

1. **CHOOSE A LISTENER.** When you know the audience you are writing for, you can start to imagine their needs, questions, objections, and level of interest. The simplest way to define this audience is by choosing a single person who is representative of this group, and write it "for him." Maybe this person can even be available to read and give feedback about your work, to help you learn if it was received as you intended.

2. **NAME THE OBJECTIVE OF WHAT YOU ARE WRITING.** If you are writing on assignment or for a client, this is where you'd articulate exactly what goals you've been hired to accomplish. If you are writing something for a themed contest or publication, define the topic or parameters within which you must perform. And if you are writing creative nonfiction, poetry, or fiction that is not driven by particular submission requirements, try setting your own standard for what you expect this piece to do/be/accomplish and then observe if this makes a difference in your writing and revising experience.

3. **WRITE!** You know everything you need to know about this, already! [This is the sound of me shaking my pom-poms.]

4. **REVISE!** Anyone who's ever spent years revising a single piece of writing knows all too well what hitting an eight-iron three hundred times might be like. Take a look at the revision tips on page 146 in this chapter if you'd like ideas to guide your process; then get out there and start swinging.

5. **EVALUATE WHETHER YOU HAVE ACHIEVED YOUR OBJECTIVE.** When your piece feels finished, revisit the goals articulated in numbers 1 and 2, and see how your writing measures up. If there are discrepancies, return to number 4, and then repeat. If you didn't hit the mark the first time, don't worry. Remember, this is all practice. And the only way we improve is through repetition. Practice shapes us, so we can most effectively give shape to our writing.

BE A PROFESSIONAL, NOT A PERFECTIONIST

> *Ring the bells that still can ring.*
> *Forget your perfect offering.*
> *There is a crack, a crack in everything.*
> *That's how the light gets in."*

> —LEONARD COHEN, *singer-songwriter, musician, poet, and novelist*

Years ago when I was single, my mother bought me a nightshirt that had an illustration of a skeleton sitting on a park bench wearing a pretty summer dress and a floppy hat with a daisy in it. The caption below this image said, "Waiting for the Perfect Man." Without going into the details of my personal life, suffice it to say that this image is one that I recall when I need a reminder about the futility of the pursuit of perfection.

I have dear friends who simply can't finish any writing project because they don't believe it will ever be good, or finished, enough. I used to be this way. If I wasn't going to be incontrovertibly perfect right out of the gate, then it wasn't worth putting writing out in the world. But that's not how life, or writing, works. At the very best, we start as decent writers and end up very good. And if we're not willing to start somewhere, work hard, and field test our work by sending it out into the world and getting feedback, we can be guaranteed stunted growth and limited productivity. This is the nature of inertia. Immobility leads to more of the same; forward motion keeps you moving forward.

My gears clicked into motion when I took off those self-punishing perfection glasses and started noticing that there were imperfect writers being published all around me, some in very impressive places. And the difference between the published writers and me was that they were putting their work out there, and I wasn't. So I decided to set my standard at *professional* instead of *perfect*, and committed to respecting my work and my evolution by doing the very best I could, bringing the utmost integrity and respect to collaborations with editors, publishers, agents, and anyone interested in presenting my work, and simply trusting the process. In doing so, I exited the dead-end alley of perfection for the open road of life as a professional writer.

You may be asking, *But what if someone doesn't like what I've written and I'm exposed as a fraud?* Let's be clear about this so you can make your peace now: Not everyone is going to like what you've written; that's the reality of the business. Even the most famous and well-paid writers are imperfect, and not one is universally admired. Remember: Your attitude is in your hands. If you can let go of the expectation of unanimous approval and hold onto your commitment to your evolution no matter what, you have a framework for managing whatever feedback you get. Be proud that you are doing your best and leave perfection on that park bench where it belongs, worried to the bone.

KNOW WHEN TO HOLD 'EM; KNOW WHEN TO FOLD 'EM

How do you know when a piece of writing is as polished as can be and ready to travel in the world without you? Following are a range of questions you can consider each time you're finishing a piece of writing to help you feel confident that you're sending out your best work. Not all of these will apply to every type of writing or its intended place of publication. Take what is useful to you and don't worry about the rest.

Revision Checklist

1. Have I completed the three-step revision process from big picture to nitty-gritty (as recommended on page 146)?

2. Have I reviewed and revised this at least three times?

3. Has this piece had time to "settle" before its final revision?

4. Have I carefully proofed for spelling, grammar, consistent verb tense, and an overall cohesive reader experience?

5. Have I done everything in my power to make the craft of this piece—language, action, imagery, dialogue, narrative arc, use of line and stanza, voice, point of view—as powerful as it can be? (I recommend that you make and use your own detailed craft checklist for your particular genre of writing, and tick off each item each time you revise to ensure that you're covering all your bases.)

6. Has this piece been read and edited by at least one (ideally three) colleague or advisor whose expertise and opinion I trust?

7. Have I run a spell-checker?

8. Have I made sure there are no strange formatting errors or page breaks?

9. Where have I said something that could be simpler or clearer?

10. Does this piece integrate and reflect the knowledge I've gained from working with (or being rejected by) this (or similar) magazine/client/literary journal in the past?

11. Does it integrate and reflect what I've learned about being productive and successful with this genre or style of writing in this type of market?

12. Does this meet stated submission guideline requirements such as word count, formatting, packaging, presentation, topic, theme, etc.?

13. Does this meet the objectives stated in my client/publication contract or my own stated creative goals?

14. Is my bio up-to-date, concise, and reflecting the tone of this opportunity?

15. Have I entered this submission into my log so I can track it effectively?

16. What does my gut say? Am I really finished, or is there more work to do here even if I'm not exactly sure what that work is yet?

When you're satisfied that your piece is publication–ready, and you're prepared to hit "send," it's time to plug into your submissions system so you can manage the trajectory of this piece in the context of the rest of your writing and publishing life. Chapter sixteen tells you how to establish a productive system that can keep your submissions on track.

And when you've finished a piece of writing, by all means, celebrate! There are no guarantees in the writing life beyond your own reliability to yourself. So you may as well set the bar high for the rest of the world by appreciating all that you have done to bring this piece to fruition. If this seems awkward to you, and most likely it will if you're not already in the habit, chapter twenty is full of ideas.

MEETING DEADLINES

I've emphasized how important it is to meet the deadlines you have promised, both to yourself and to others. And I've proposed a wide range of strategies and systems for managing the various steps of

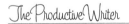

accomplishing this. Let's take a quick look at the composite. Consider this high-level list your success strategy overview, for which you'll use the various approaches explored in this book to execute:

- Have a highly visible system that shows you clearly what is due and when. Ideally, you'll be looking at the big picture of all of your upcoming deadlines at one time so you can prioritize time and energy in meeting them all effectively.
- Clearly spell out the scope of what you agreed to deliver, so you can measure your writing against that objective each step of the way.
- Create clear accountability for yourself to ensure that you will be motivated to meet each deadline.
- Map out a schedule that shows you how and when you have the hours to cross the finish line. (Even if you don't follow the schedule, seeing without a doubt that it can be done in the hours you have is powerful motivation.)
- Claim your carrot: Know what you're writing this for and what value it will bring you.
- Honor your rhythms. Write when you are most effective, whenever possible; and give yourself space to do other productivity-enhancing work when you are less effective.
- Reward yourself with something simple and pleasurable—a walk, a visit with a friend, a book you've been wanting—when you meet your deadline.
- Update your various logs, files, and systems with whatever you'd like to reference from this project in the future, whether that's templates, lessons learned, repurposed content, submission/publication details, or what you feared and overcame.
- Celebrate all that you appreciate about your accomplishment and the work you did to get there.

Chapter 16

PUBLISHING AND LANDING GIGS

THE PRODUCTIVE WRITER PUBLISHING SUCCESS FORMULA:

- Stand on your own solid ground before you start sending out work.
- Write and revise to the best of your ability.
- Do your due diligence to place your work in the right hands and publications, or pitch/bid on the right gigs.
- Know what you are worth.
- Create and maintain a submission system.
- Target your markets.
- Write queries and bids that connect.
- Measure performance against goals.
- Be willing to work through rejection, learn, and evolve.

Publishing is an alchemy of hard work (yours), subjective judging (editors'/publishers'/clients'/agents'), and luck (that part's up to the universe).

Let's consider your part of the bargain. As I see it, your publishing priorities should include:

- Carefully crafting your work.
- Thoroughly researching markets.
- Writing cover letters or queries that connect.
- Building relationships with publishing partners and/or clients over time.

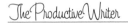

- Establishing a process for sending your work out regularly.

VALIDATION IS GOOD, TRUST IN YOURSELF IS BETTER

External validation can be quite helpful, but it has nothing to do with who we are as writers or people. Each affirming nod from the folks in the business of publishing becomes a stepping stone to the next possibility. Publication, pay, awards, and other recognition can make us feel pretty good (or rich or important) for a short period of time. But often, they don't feel as good as we think they might, or for as long as we would hope.

This is because the way the external world sees us is not a viable foothold for how we feel about ourselves. Dependency on third-party approval is shaky, unreliable ground. Hanging your hat, your identity, or your self-esteem on such affirmation is as good an idea as living on a bridge. Your relationship with your writing is the most solid ground you have. The more you dedicate yourself to developing your skill, bolstering your writing practice, and fortifying your platform, the more stable you will become in the ever-changing winds of public opinion. And I'd suggest waiting to attempt publishing until you feel that solid ground of inner-Productive-Writer-authority under your feet.

Once you're fairly certain that you and your writing will withstand a good gust of rejection, it's time to start sending out your work for publication. When the recognition, rewards, and rejections come, you'll cross the bridge to wherever they lead you, stand on the solid ground of your intrinsically valuable writing life, and go on to write the next edifice and the next.

SEND YOUR BEST WORK

Easier said than done, right? Not if you've read chapter fifteen of this book! Commit to professionalism (vs. perfectionism), use your own craft- or platform-centric version of the proofing checklist, don't push too hard to get across the finish line, trust your inner editor, and you'll be as prepared as you can possibly be to send your work out for consideration.

KNOW WHAT YOU ARE WORTH

In chapter seven, you'll find a process for tracking time so you can start to understand how much writing you are able to accomplish per hour. This can help you determine if a writing opportunity is offering a pay rate that is reasonable for you. And in situations where you are bidding on work for a client, it will help you estimate your time and costs effectively.

The more complicated question is: What is your time and your work worth to you? To answer this, you may want to consider the following:

- Research market rates in your area or your field. Learn what other teachers are charging for classes of similar duration, or what other freelance writers are billing. If you are seeking publication in a magazine, compare pay rates for publications of similar scope or size.
- Are you a beginner or an expert in your field or on your topic? The more proven experience under your belt, the higher you are likely to be paid. Explore the range available for a given project, and estimate realistically where your pay rate might fall.
- What is the non-monetary value of this opportunity? For example, if the pay for a project is lower than you would like but you could gain a valuable clip or portfolio piece, or improve your visibility in a way that will help you establish a foothold and reputation in your writing specialty, is the project worth doing?
- How does this opportunity express your goals and values to grow your platform, have fun, evolve, become proficient in this market/topic/field, or [plug in your priority here]?
- What does your gut say?

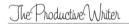

The more experience you have publishing and/or selling your work to clients, the more confidence you will have, both in the value of what you are offering and in the fact that you are pricing it right. For now, take it slowly, do your due diligence, and commit to learning as you go about what you are willing to write, for what pay, and other, less tangible but equally valid rewards.

HOW TO ESTABLISH A SUBMISSION SYSTEM

The easier it is to send your work out for publication, the more likely you are to do it. Over the years, I have kept both paper and computer files that help me put everything I need to write or submit a poem for publication at my fingertips. I recommend establishing a single flexible system that's easy to reach (right on your desk or your computer desktop) and lets you easily add/remove categories and material over time.

Soft Copies
Try creating a single "Publishing" folder in your computer with subfolders for the categories on the next page.

Hard Copies
Ideally, you'll have all of your hard copies in a single, easily accessible place, such as a three-ring binder or a paper file stand on your desk. Within that system, you'll have tabs or folders for the categories on the next page.

Set up (or update) your system this week, and you'll be thanking yourself for the rest of the year, and the rest of your writing and publishing days.

On the following page are some of the categories I've used. Use whatever pleases you and/or applies to your genres(s) of writing, add whatever is missing for your particular approach, and make your system your own.

KNOWING THE STATUS OF YOUR PUBLISHING PROCESS AT A GLANCE

SECTION NAME	CONTENTS
Great Quotes	Collect quotes that inspire you—about writing as well as any other themes that attract you. Often a quote will spark a poem. Or I'll realize after writing a poem that a certain snippet of wisdom would make the perfect epigraph.
Inspiration	I save my favorite writing here and refer to it often. In fact, I have subcategories within this big one for poetry, fiction, and nonfiction. These remind me what's possible in my writing life, and they can give me a jump-start when my writing is stuck.
Acorns	It's helpful to designate one easy-to-access place where you can compile and easily reference your "acorns" (ideas, inspirations, and writing snippets that will later grow into great strong oaks of finished pieces).
Writing in the Works	All drafts that are still taking shape live here. Most of my work spends some time ripening in this folder. When I sit down with my editor hat on, I generally have a selection of in-the-works writing to choose from.
Finished Pieces	Keep your finished work that's ready to go public here, but don't let it burn a hole in your folder! Find the right places to submit, then send it.
Contests and Publication	File submissions requirements and deadlines for contests and literary journals in one place, organized by submission date. And/or, if you are targeting particular magazines, track editorial calendar themes/topics here and plan to time your submissions accordingly. This will act as a reminder so you don't miss opportunities to submit your work.
Submission Log	Use a handwritten list, Word table, or Excel spreadsheet to track when and where you queried or submitted your work, and whether it was accepted. Make note of any personal correspondence you receive from editors so you can follow up effectively with the next query or submission. (This is the most important tool! More details are provided below.)

Published Writing	Keep a list (and a digital copy, print copy, and online link, if available) of your pieces published and the publications/dates in which they appear. This will help you keep your bio up to date with all of your latest accomplishments and avoid sending something out that's already been published. Flip through this file whenever you need a publishing pick-me-up. (I also recommend dedicating a special place in your home to showcasing publications in which your work appears. But this is less for your publishing process and more to enjoy and celebrate your successes.)
Friends' Writing	Sharing work with friends and colleagues can help inspire and motivate your own writing practice. I like to revisit friends' writing and admire its evolution over time.
Cover Letter and Bio	Keep both a template with the latest/greatest info and an archive of past cover letters and bios so that you always have the info you need at your fingertips when it's time to send in a submission.
Submission Possibilities	This can include a list of links to URLs of online journals and/or a collection of print publications—those I admire and to which I may submit in the future.

MANAGING SUBMISSIONS: USE A LOG

Of all of the categories above, the most important tool you'll need for your publishing system is a submission log. Use either a handwritten list, Word table, or Excel spreadsheet to track when and where you submitted your work, and whether it was accepted.

Your spreadsheet will be most effective if it tracks the following:

- Name of publication
- Name of contest or issue for which you are querying or submitting
- Payment range or prize money (if applicable)
- Titles of each piece of work sent
- Submission deadline
- Date sent

- Response deadline (if one is promised by the publication)
- Results (note if your work was published or rejected)
- Notes: Record any special submission requirements or personal correspondence you receive from editors so you can follow up effectively with the next query or submission.

TARGET YOUR MARKETS

But how do you know where to send your work? Researching target publications, markets, or clients will help you understand where to place and how to pitch what you're offering.

If you commit to steadily building a case for your future, as advised in chapter one, when it comes time to find a home for your writing, you will already have a file overflowing with inspired ideas about publications or opportunities that seem promising. If you are starting from scratch and seeking to publish creative writing or magazine articles, you'll want to use a reputable and comprehensive resource for learning about publications that could be a fit for you. Once you have made a list of possibilities, thoroughly investigate them to confirm that they are a fit. Writer's Digest Books offers a wide selection of titles covering the full spectrum of creative and business writing publication opportunities, plus a great online resource, WritersMarket.com, where you can do comprehensive market searches.

QUERIES AND BIDS THAT CONNECT

Consider these big-picture suggestions when you are querying or bidding on a writing project:

- **DO YOUR HOMEWORK.** Make sure that you clearly understand the ethos, spirit, and objectives of the organization or publication you are pitching.

- **UNDERSTAND YOUR FIT.** Be realistic with yourself and appraise exactly how your platform, skills, experience, contacts (should there be interviews or collaborations required), and goals line up with the opportunity available.
- **CONNECT THE DOTS.** In your pitch or query, be clear about how your solution specifically addresses the need that you are proposing to solve, and why you are the ideal person to deliver such a solution.

In short, your queries and bids should leave the recipient convinced that she's found the person for the job, at a great value. For specific details about how to write a high-impact query, check out Wendy Burt-Thomas's *The Writer's Digest Guide to Query Letters*. There you'll find everything you need to know about navigating these waters productively. Chapter seventeen will prepare you for a productive and prosperous relationship with the editors and clients who hire you.

MEASURING PERFORMANCE AGAINST GOALS

In chapter four, you set specific goals for your Productive Writing life. If literary publishing or magazine or business writing were on that list, your submission log is a great way to measure how you're doing. Keep your log up-to-date and review it at least every month so you can learn over time where you're getting the most traction for your efforts. Commit to continuously refining your approach, and you will learn how to be more and more effective in getting the results you want.

BE WILLING TO WORK THROUGH REJECTION, LEARN, AND EVOLVE

Rejection is success in sheep's clothing. It is the chafe that softens you to the supple and receptive writer that you need to be to keep on getting better and working harder, no matter what.

When we lean into the turn on a motorcycle, even the hairpin curves are survivable. When we lean into a rejection with friendly interest, a relentless appreciation for our courage to submit and submit again, and a willingness to refine both our work and our approach based on what the editors say, we are showing up all buttoned up for success, with neon arrows and flashing lights that say, "Find me here."

Chapter 17

SUSTAINING MEANINGFUL RELATIONSHIPS

BOTH THE BUSINESS AND PRACTICE OF WRITING HAVE AT their foundation meaningful and productive relationships. Why? Because relationships are the waters on which our writing craft travel. We may write alone, but what we write and how we share it are ultimately entwined in the relationships we have—and those we intend to create. Let's consider why these are important, and how to make them as productive as they can be.

YOUR COMMUNITY IS YOUR POT OF GOLD

Without people to share ideas with, learn from, explore opportunities with, and offer our writing to, we are in monologue. And that only gets us so far. By entering a dialogue, a relationship, a community, we blow the doors of possibility wide open. We learn what's resonating with others in our writing and where our opportunities for improvement may be. We hear about a teaching or publishing opportunity from a friend. We connect with an agent because we knew to attend the conference where she would be. We get invited to speak about our area of expertise because there are people out there who are familiar with our platform and want to hear about it. (And we give generously to our community: encouragement, referrals, testimonials, feedback, a shoulder to lean on, and whatever else is asked that we can afford to give.)

Quite simply, we feel a part of the larger conversation of our writing lives because we have lifted our heads from our own personal page to exchange wisdom and encouragement through the dance of relationship. Your writing community is your bedrock. It gives you strength, courage, information, support, validation, encouragement, celebration, and motivation to keep on plugging.

A Community of Two: Your Writing Buddy

"Community" can be a big and abstract, and slightly unapproachable, concept. If the thought of creating one sounds daunting to you, let's start with something far simpler: a friend. Having a single person you can count on to care about your writing life and share her own may be more important than any skill or system you can put into effect. Why? Because when we have a generous witness, we are more powerful and possible. When we are in process with someone who has similar passions and aspirations, the momentum we generate can be bigger and more fun.

For my formative poetry years, my friend Sebastian Ellis's enthusiasm about poetry—and my work in particular—helped me understand what I valued about my own writing. And for the thirteen years that I've been a marketing communications consultant, I have spoken nearly every day to my former business partner, now colleague and dear friend, Pamela Kim. She is often my first reader, my best critic, an idea-generation collaborator, and a brilliant guide and companion in the life of productive writing.

Find people you care about, whose writing you like. Accompany them on their journey, and invite them to accompany you on yours.

How to Establish and Grow a Writing Community

A writing community develops over time. It is comprised of the people you enjoy who share your interest in writing and publishing: friends, classmates, and colleagues. There are endless ways to go about getting connected. Here are a few.

- **PARTICIPATE IN LITERARY EVENTS.** You may meet these folks through writing or critique groups, workshops, conferences, readings, your kids' school, and other events in your community. Check your local newspaper, literary calendar, library and community bulletin boards for news of such happenings. Or try visiting www.meetup.com, then plug in your genre or writing topic of interest to see if there's an opportunity to connect with people who share your passion.

- **CREATE YOUR OWN COMMUNITY CONTEXT.** If you can't find an event or opportunity to connect with other writers where you live, start one or travel to one.

- **PUT YOURSELF OUT THERE.** When you attend events, talk to the people around you. Ask questions of the presenters, give thanks to the hosts and facilitators, sign up for mailing lists, exchange contact info, and find out what you can do to get involved.

- **GIVE SERVICE.** This may be the most satisfying way to plug into your writing community. Host a lecture or literary event. (Chapter seventy-nine in my book *Writing the Life Poetic* tells you how.) Find an institution such as a nursing home or homeless shelter in your community where people have limited access to writing opportunities, and share your love of the word with them. Create an e-zine (a newsletter or magazine distributed via e-mail) that shares writing from you and/or your community. As you tune in to what's already available for writers where you live, you are likely to start imagining new ways to add value.

- **FIND THE RIGHT FIT FOR YOU.** If you join a group and it doesn't feel right for whatever reason, trust yourself and move on quickly. You know who and what resonates for you. And most likely you can quickly evaluate if a community context is moving you forward or holding you back. I have friends who have been discouraged by joining writing critique groups where clearly their work and their spirit was not a fit with the general vibe of the group. Don't worry, it's a big world and there are many other groups to explore. And if you can't find one that fits just right, start one and shape it to your own standards.

- **REMEMBER THAT IT'S ALL YOUR WRITING LIFE!** What better way to cultivate your community than by inviting the people around you to share their wisdom? Talk to people. Leave the house. Do a little qualitative research. Consider everyone you meet a source of ideas, stories, and insights, and you'll build a lasting bridge between your "real life" and your "writing life."

GUIDES CAN HELP SHOW YOU THE WAY

Role models remind us what is possible, keep us reaching higher, and sometimes even offer valuable blueprints for how we might attempt what they have accomplished. Chapter one suggests that you pay attention to your writing heroes online to get an impression of what's possible in your own writing life.

Another, more structured option is to take a class or a workshop with a writer you admire. Some teachers also offer individualized coaching or editing; this gives you the opportunity for continued mentorship and guidance if the fit is right. Get a referral from someone in your writing community, if you can. Your goal should be making sure that you're learning with someone whose spirit and teaching style (as well as expertise) is aligned with your temperament and learning style. If you feel challenged, encouraged, and safe, chances are you're in the right learning environment for you.

Plus, remember that with this book in your hands, you've already chosen a powerful and affordable form of guidance. You could continue on this path and give yourself a thorough education in the possibilities of the writing life through the abundance of literature available on every topic imaginable—from craft to platform to publishing to promotion— letting authors be your guides.

BUSINESS PARTNERS CAN HELP BRING YOUR WORK FORWARD

> *I see this over and over again: A writer early in her career who regards her agent as a badge of legitimacy, or a key to kingdom of New York Publishing, and who therefore neglects the vital fact that they are the talent..."*

—STEVE ALMOND, *author of* Candyfreak

Selling and publishing writing is always a collaboration—whether you're doing it for a client or a publication. A writer's business partners are likely to be editors, agents, publishers, and businesses or magazines that pay for writing.

Two things are true when you are working with an editor or a client: Your ideas, talent, hard work, and fabulous writing create the content that helps keep the wheels of their enterprise turning. And you are in service to their objectives, a vessel of copy through which their needs are met. Your job is to deliver what you have agreed to, in the voice of that particular company or publication, when appropriate.

This means that you check your ego at the door, and you train your metaphors and proof points to jump higher than the benchmarks, without going over word count. Your job is to become the voice of the story you have been hired to tell. And when you are asked to revise and change direction, you smile and do so until everyone is satisfied (within whatever scope was originally established, of course. For example, if you agreed to two rounds of revision at a certain pay rate, it's time to renegotiate payment if you are asked for additional edits.)

Likewise, when you are writing a nonfiction book, you are sharing your expertise in your own way, but you are doing so within an agreed-upon structure, voice, and style that has been negotiated and agreed upon with your publisher in advance. Poetry and fiction are slightly different in that a full-length manuscript (or individual poem or story) is typically written first, and then accepted for publication. But you can still expect an editorial process in which creative work is refined collaboratively with the publication's editor.

How to Collaborate Productively With Business Partners

PARTNER	LEARN THEIR EXPECTATIONS	COMMUNICATE YOUR NEEDS
Editor	• What is my final deliverable deadline? • In what format should I present my work? • How closely do you want me to stick to our agreed outline/TOC /scope of work? • How do you give feedback? • Do you want to see my revisions red-lined? • How many rounds of revision should I expect? • Are there any red-alert issues you can see from here that I should pay special attention to (such as permissions)? • How and when will feedback be communicated?	• Communicate your rate and agree to terms that work for you and the editor. • Sign a contract that makes these terms clear. • Communicate your timing needs and any other requirements that define your participation in the project.

Client	Collaboratively define with the client their: • Objectives • Deadlines • Budget • Timeline/expected number of drafts • Desired voice/tone • Available source information • Pay rate and schedule	• Create or request a thorough creative brief signed by both parties. • Ensure that everyone agrees to a clear schedule for writing, editing, and finalizing copy. • Feedback per the schedule—on time. • Payment terms: on what dates or stages in the process you expect to be paid.

Agent	• What topics and genres do you represent?
	
	 • How do you like to be approached by writers?
	
	 • How do you prefer to receive queries and submissions?
		• Send a query (and proposal if there is interest) that tell a compelling story about your project and your platform on this topic.
		
		 • If the agent is interested in representing you:
		
		   • Articulate the type of support and frequency of contact you desire.
		
		   • Define your goals for your current project/long-term career.

READERS CAN BRING YOU BUZZ CURRENCY

Until you start publishing widely, you are not likely to know who your readers actually are or what they expect from you. Your job until that time comes is to simply choose an imagined reader (to help yourself stay on track with your writing focus), be yourself, and stay true to whatever platform, goals, and ideals you have set for yourself.

Along your way, if you pay attention to the feedback you get as your work becomes more and more visible, you'll start to get a feel for what kinds of people are attracted to what you write, and you'll understand better and better how you are meeting their needs. (Blogging can be very useful in this process, as it's a forum for "publishing" your own work instantly and getting reader feedback through the comments.) Through your readers' eyes and buzz, you will start to see what you're doing more clearly—whether you agree or not with how your work is being represented. As this groundswell is building over the years, I invite you to simply be grateful for any buzz you get and to consider yourself a student of your readers. Let them teach you about what is needed, how you are fulfilling that need, and if there is anything else you can do (and are interested in doing) to answer the call.

HONOR YOURSELF, HONOR YOUR RELATIONSHIPS

> As smoking is to the lungs, so is resentment to the soul; even one puff is bad for you."

—ELIZABETH GILBERT, *author of* Eat Pray Love

Set Realistic Expectations—Then Deliver on Them

A writer's word is her reputation. The best way to build productive, long-term relationships for any project is to leave no doubt about what is expected, how it will be accomplished, by when, by whom, and at what cost—and then to deliver on those promises flawlessly. And if the creek does rise and you are not able to do what you have promised, renegotiate responsibly as early in the process as possible, so your client doesn't end up in that creek with you—but without a paddle.

Use Envy as a Compass

Let us assume that you are in the company of an incredible community of productive writers who are all working hard and having success. Sooner or later, someone is going to accomplish something that will

pluck one of your "no fair, that was meant for ME!" heartstrings. In this way, envy is an extremely useful indicator of desire. We may not even know we are wanting something until that chord plays through us.

I'm going to let you in on a secret: There is enough to go around. When good things happen to people you know, let that be a sign that good things are coming for you, too. If you see someone out there doing something you want and you feel envious, why not simply appreciate the valuable information this gives you about your own goals and desires? Let envy be your jet fuel. Then get back to work.

LET SUCCESS BE CONTAGIOUS

Okay, now you've harnessed envy to your advantage and so have the people around you. It's time to start seriously tuning into each other's success. We tend to absorb the juices we're simmering in. If you're cooking in a pot spiced with the good news of your writing community, chances are you're going to fill up with that energy and start creating some of your own. And vice versa. So don't hesitate to let the people around you know about your successes. And when you hear the good news of others, drink it in like water and let it help you grow.

Be Grateful

Gratitude is the glue of relationships. I am a devotee of the handwritten thank-you note because it slows me down to really consider what I appreciate about the person I am writing to, and it gives me an intimate way to let her know. When you appreciate your colleagues, business partners, and community at-large for the contributions they make to your writing life, you are fortifying a bond that feels good to everyone involved. The person who gets the phone call or handwritten letter will remember that working with you is a rewarding experience.

Chapter 18

GOING PUBLIC

THE PRODUCTIVE WRITER MAKES A SPLASH IN PUBLIC BY:

- Preparing well.
- Dressing for success.
- Offering something of value that listeners want (and sending them home with something memorable).
- Being authentic.
- Managing fear.
- Expressing gratitude.

We write alone, but when we offer our work to the world, we enter a larger conversation. Whether it is live events, workshops, readings, or online communities and forums, find a place to go where you can practice saying, "This is who I am, and this is what I write." As you practice publicly, your private, behind-the-curtain voice will grow more sure and confident. As you present your work to listeners, you will learn more about what you know, what you're writing, and who is interested in it.

PRODUCTIVE PRESENTATION MATERIALS

Nothing boosts confidence and eases anxiety like thorough preparation. Give yourself the best possible chance of success when you get in

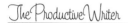

front of an audience by arriving with content and materials that are suited for your event and most likely to connect with participants.

Define Objectives of Event

Before you sit down to prepare for your event, define its objectives and parameters:

- **TYPE OF EVENT:** Is this a lecture? A workshop? Reading? What type of experience are you creating?
- **CONTEXT/SETTING:** What is the spirit or tone or orientation of the organization through which you are presenting? Formal, quirky, relaxed, religious?
- **AUDIENCE NEEDS:** What type of people will you be speaking to? Beginning poets? Ph.D. mathematicians? What kind of information are they seeking?
- **TOPIC:** What is the scope of the topic you will be offering to meet this need?
- **TIME FRAME:** How long does the event run?

Create a Detailed Outline: For a Lecture or Workshop

- Like any good expository writing, make sure the experience you are creating has a main idea, at least three supporting points, and lots of clear and engaging examples to bring it all to life.
- Use 14-point font or larger so you can easily read content without losing your place.
- Make key points short and easy to comprehend at a glance.
- Provide as much backup detail as you need—err on the side of overpreparing here.
- If you are weaving in exercises, make a note about how much time you should allow each exercise so you don't have to remember off the cuff (then make sure to bring a timepiece).

Prepare for Contingencies

- Know what you will cut (and indicate this on your outline in a way that is clear to you) if you are running slow and likely to go over your time limit.
- Have at least a few additional points and/or exercises on hand as backup, in case things go more quickly than planned.

Organize Any Auxiliary Literature You'll Reference

- If you'll be reading from books or documents not included in your handy outline, make sure to have these in the order of appearance, with key pages or content tabbed, highlighted, or referenced in whatever way will be most easy for you to find and read.
- Keep such referencing to a minimum. Whenever possible, include excerpts from other pieces of writing directly in your outline so you can stay focused on your presentation and not get lost in shuffling books and paper.

Bring Handouts for Participants

- Always bring handouts to share with participants. People like going home with something useful that reinforces what they've learned. Handouts can cover additional information related to your presentation, recap key points, offer resources or exercises or tips or whatever will reinforce the live experience while adding a little extra value.
- Make sure the materials you provide are clear, easy to read, and produced professionally.
- Always handle reproduction of handouts yourself; they are a reflection of you, so make sure they look great. I once made the mistake of allowing a generous and well-meaning organization (for whom I was speaking) to make copies of my materials, and I was embarrassed to have my name on the results.

- Ask what the maximum expected number of attendees is, and bring 10 percent more handouts
- Provide your name and contact information on every page, so folks will remember you as they refer to your materials – and contact you if they are interested in learning more.
- Unless you're distributing exercises that will be done together during the course of your presentation, wait to share handouts until you are finished. When folks have papers to look at while a speaker is speaking, they may get distracted and pay less attention than you would like.
- Rather than leave them on a table in the back of the room, distribute handouts yourself. That way, you'll be sure everyone gets one.

Rehearse and Refine

- Read your presentation out loud, all the way through, to a supportive listener.
- Notice where you get stuck, where information is bumpy, where you're going on too long.
- Notice where you feel confident and where you feel shaky.
- Measure timing to make sure it matches the event's timing.
- Practice answering audience questions.
- Ask your listener to give you feedback about his experience. Specifically, you will want feedback on: tone, pacing, what's engaging and what's not.
- Based on your own observations and the feedback of your listener, refine your presentation (and practice again) as many times as you need until you feel confident about the material and your ability to deliver it.

Archive for the Next Time

Once you have your first public presentation under your belt, you have a wealth of knowledge about what worked and what didn't. When you get home from your event, while the experience is fresh, make notes on your outline to this effect so you can remember what should be repeated and what can be refined for next time. Then file it somewhere where it will be easy to find the next time you're getting ready to speak. (Chapter nine tells all about effective filing.) The next time you're going public, you'll have a solid starting place. If you repeat this evaluation/archive process each time you present on this topic, your performance and results are sure to improve exponentially every time.

Rules for Reading Creative Work

- Prepare a list of pieces (or a section of a longer piece) you will read, and an order for them.
- Organize books, papers, or materials in an order that will be easiest to reference.
- Consider any introductions or anecdotes you'd like to share about each piece before presenting it. Maybe even take a few notes to guide you.
- Make sure the documents you're reading from are legible. (I've seen many a reader get up to read a published piece, only to find that the font is too small to easily read it.)
- Practice in front of a supportive listener. Get feedback about how you look, sound, and feel. Ask about where they were tuned in and tuned out.
- Make any modifications to materials based on length of time and your listener's feedback.
- Continue practicing and refining until you feel at ease.

PUBLIC APPEARANCE READY-TO-GO SUPPLY KIT

Knowing you're equipped with everything you could possibly need at a public event will give you a foundation of confidence. Use this checklist (whatever parts of it pertain to you) to prepare when you're going

to be reading, speaking, or teaching publicly, and know that you'll walk in the door on solid ground.

- **ROLLING FILE CART THAT FOLDS FOR STORAGE.** With a mobile file cart that wheels and lifts easily, you can travel to and from each event with everything you need. Ideally, you will use this cart to store all of the stuff listed below in between events so you have them on hand when you need them without having to prepare too much each time you take the show on the road.

- **PRESENTATION INVENTORY LIST.** Make a list of everything you want to have on hand each time you're in front of an audience. (Many of the items to follow in this section may appear on your list.) Keep it taped on the lid of your rolling file cart or on the wall above where you store it for easy reference. Check to make sure you have everything you need each time you take your show on the road.

- **SOMETHING YOU'VE WRITTEN** that you can send home with folks. Whether it's a nicely photocopied essay or article or poem, a chapbook or a book, make sure you have something to either give away or sell. I am an optimist. I try to bring at least 20 percent more than expected demand at any given event. A few times, I've been grateful that I did. (If you've traveled by car, it can't hurt to have a big box of extras stashed in the backseat, just in case.) You will learn over time what kind of supply to bring depending on the type of event you're doing. Your inventory list below will help you measure over time.

- **A NON-SMEARING PEN** to autograph whatever you are giving away or selling. I like fine-point Sharpies. Experiment to find the pen that is most comfortable and aesthetically pleasing to you.

- **A SECOND PEN THAT YOU DON'T MIND LOSING** for your mailing list. This pen sits out unsupervised and hopefully will be used by many people. More often than not, it will disappear. Make sure you're not attached to this one.
- **A FEW STANDARD GREETINGS FOR AUTOGRAPHING.** When you have a line of people winding through an auditorium waiting for signatures (we should all be so lucky), you don't want to get tripped up wondering what to write for each person and keep folks waiting.

  I have three different messages I tend to repeat and personalize a bit depending on if and what I know about the person buying the book. Practice a few different greetings at home and have them in mind when it's time to sign so you can save your energy for connecting with the person in front of you.
- **BUSINESS CARDS** with all of the contact info you'd like the general public to have, including your e-mail address, website, blog, and possibly a P.O. Box. (It's not a great idea to share your home address with the general public. If you want to invite snail mail, a P.O. Box for your writing life is a good compromise.) Ideally, the card will visually reflect (with a logo, photograph, illustration, font or color choice) the spirit of who you are and what you write so that people associate it with you at first glance, even before reading it.
- **MAILING LIST.** Make your mailing list visible at every event, actively invite people to sign it, and be sure to offer a compelling reward for signing, such as a free e-book or an e-zine subscription. And make the list attractive and eye-catching so folks will notice it—and be inspired to sign. Mine has artwork from my book cover.

- **PROMOTIONAL GIVEAWAYS** such as bookmarks, pens, etc. This is an important one. People like free stuff. You'll get noticed if you have something fun, attractive, useful (or all of the above) to share. Make sure everything you give away has your contact information on it and an enticing phrase about who you are and what you do. I have three different bookmarks with images and little snippets of wisdom from my book. People gobble them up.

- **INVENTORY LIST.** If you are selling books or chapbooks or CDs at an event, you should always know how many you have on hand and how many you sold. A simple, handwritten inventory list can help you keep track of sales at each event. This record will not only enable accurate accounting for tax purposes, but will also teach you over time about the purchasing trends of your audience at various types of events.

- **CASH BOX AND CHANGE**—or envelope with multiple denomination bills for making change. (Always note how much cash you're starting with so you have a clear record of earnings at the end of the event.)

- **FLYERS OR BROCHURES WITH INFORMATION ABOUT UPCOMING EVENTS OR CLASSES.** Fold one into every book you sell and include it with every promotional giveaway. You always want folks to know what you're offering, where they can find you online, and when they can connect with you next in person.

- **DISPLAYS FOR FLYERS AND ANYTHING YOU MIGHT BE SELLING.** Inexpensive at any office supply store.

- **VISIBLE AND ATTRACTIVE COST INFO.** Display detailing the cost of anything you are selling. (Mine says "Buy Happiness!" and features the image of each book, along with a discounted price for purchasing two together.) Make it attractive and appealing, too.

- **MORAL AND PRACTICAL SUPPORT.** Have a friendly and well-spoken friend represent you, sell your books, offer information, and answer questions while you are speaking or reading. He can also smile up at you from the audience to put you at ease.

- **FREE, USEFUL INFORMATION THAT IS RELEVANT TO THIS EVENT/ AUDIENCE.** For example, I offer a three-page list of online and local poetry resources. And often I send workshop participants home with extra tips and exercises not covered in class that they can do themselves at home.

- **TISSUES.** It's Murphy's law. Your nose will run when you least expect it, or you'll choke up when a participant shares her poem. Be prepared to wipe.

- **BOTTLE OF WATER.** Dry mouth is no fun when you're talking for an hour.

- **HAIR MANAGEMENT STUFF**: clips, headband and hairbrush.

- **GLASSES, IF NECESSARY.** I've watched folks juggle their bifocals, putting them on while reading and then taking them off while speaking to audiences. Do this if it works for you, but know that if you find it distracting, so will your audience. If you need to, practice at home how you will both read and connect with listeners without having to fumble around too much.

- **TIMEPIECE** so you can make sure you're staying on topic, on time, and respecting whatever parameters have been set for your event.

- **TWO COPIES OF YOUR PRESENTATION MATERIALS**: one in the rolling file box, one in your hand or purse/briefcase/etc.

- **AN INSCRIBED COPY OF WHATEVER YOU ARE GIVING AWAY OR SELLING FOR THE EVENT HOST.** Nothing says thank you like a gift of writing.

- **CAMERA.** You'll be happy to have a record of an event in images. Ask your trusty friend to photograph you in action, as well as the audience. If possible, record the event by posing with the host, attendees, and other writers/authors sharing the stage.
- **FIRST AID SUPPLIES.** A headache, allergy attack, or bleeding thumb can put a damper on a public appearance. Having some basic first aid supplies on hand can make sure that minor maladies don't get in your way when presenting. You'll appreciate having Band-aids, medications, or homeopathic remedies on hand to keep you feeling clear-headed and comfortable should you need them.
- **VIDEO OR AUDIO RECORDING.** Share your event with a wider audience by recording it and posting it on your blog or website.

HOLD YOUR FOCUS AND AUDIENCE ATTENTION

Avoid Wardrobe Malfunctions

Being dressed right can keep you in your body, grounded and present for your audience. When you get up there in front of an audience, you want to be comfortable and warm (but not too warm), in shoes that you can trust to not trip you or turn your ankle. And you want to feel attractive and confident about how you look.

Beware of dangly, jangly jewelry as this can create distracting noise and glinting light for audience members. You also want to make sure your clothes will stay in place and not require your attention—unwieldy scarves and plunging necklines can become real problems. I once went to a reading in a dress that I believed to be solidly made and found out after the fact that a slip would have been a fine idea. And at a recent reading (after writing the first draft of this chapter, I might add), I wore a large and lovely shawl that became a liability when I visited the ladies room. I hope this will spare you such embarrassments.

Breathe

Nervous about going public? Repeat after me: *Fear is just a feeling. You will survive it. And be stronger for it.* It's easy to get out of your body when you're about to do something scary. And it's important to call yourself back in to your body so you have a strong voice and feet on the ground to deliver your fine experience in a meaningful way. Chapter eleven offers a range of strategies for managing fear. Take a look, take some deep breaths, and know that the only way through fear is by having the courage to try, risk looking goofy (and—let's face it, occasionally looking goofy), get to the other side, and then keep practicing, trusting that you will improve along the way.

Be Yourself

I used to have the completely unreasonable expectation that when I stood up in front of people, I would have to pretend to be some kind of infallible expert, free of human vulnerability and failings. In short, I thought I was supposed to try to be someone other than who I was: an extremely nervous-to-be-standing-in-front-of-people, shy person who wanted very much to be liked, who compensated for insecurity by being overprepared and who sometimes spontaneously cries, stumbles, and cracks herself up when reading her own poems and the poems of others. What I learned along the way was that it was exactly those parts of me that I imagined to be most problematic that allowed me to connect with and enjoy the people I was speaking to. They actually seemed to *enjoy* my most embarrassing flaws.

The paradox is that those very "flaws" you are trying to iron out of your public persona are the greatest opportunities to make a human connection with listeners. Be yourself; that's the person they came to see.

If you straightjacket yourself into some idea of what a presentation is supposed to be, you'll miss out on the experience of having an authentic experience and a real connection with your audience. Be sincere, bring in humor if you can (you may be funnier than you think), respect and hold space for your vulnerability, and you and your audience will have the best possible chances of enjoying each other.

THE SQUEAKY WHEEL DOESN'T GET INVITED BACK

My book wasn't available at the bookstore of a conference where I was teaching. It was supposed to be there. It wasn't. I was presenting in less than an hour. And it was too late to get the book now. So, what would be the point of bringing this to anyone's attention?

Don't Be Prissy, Be Prepared

Fortunately, I was prepared for the above emergency; I had a box of books on hand and I sold them directly to workshop participants, with a personal signature, right after the event. And in so doing, I sold far more books than I likely would have if folks had to traipse across a giant convention center to find my books in the bookstore. You should always be prepared to turn disappointment into opportunity. If other people have promised to handle some part of your public experience, be prepared to handle it yourself—just in case.

Prevent Techno-Nonsense

Two years in a row, I presented at a conference; and two years in a row, I had trouble with the projector I needed for my presentation. Sometimes you just can't avoid such techno-nonsense, but often you can. I recommend that you:

- Make sure your handheld advancer for your PowerPoint presentation works by testing batteries and practicing before leaving for the event.

- Read the letter from the event organizer to make sure you have highlighted all of your to-dos and to-brings.
- Make sure you understand what kind of adaptors and connection cords you will need for your computer to speak to a projector or other audiovisual equipment; make sure you have the right ones for your computer, then bring them.
- If at all possible, practice making the connection between your equipment and others' prior to the moment when it really counts.

BE GRATEFUL

After you've presented or spoken to a group of people, think about how you can both show your appreciation and continue the dialogue with the folks in attendance long after you've left the podium. In chapter seventeen, we considered the value of gratitude in building relationships. In this chapter, we'll explore the how-to's of communicating appreciation.

Following is a recommended protocol for a gratitude wrap-up following any event. This is my list; over time, you can experiment with what works for you and create a system of your own.

- **SEND A THANK-YOU NOTE TO THE HOST.** Handwritten notes are always a surprising pleasure for folks to receive in these times of rampant virtual communication. Choose an image or message on the card that reflects the spirit of who you are and what you write. You can even print your own stationery; that's what I do.
- **SEND A PERSONALIZED THANK-YOU NOTE TO EVERYONE YOU KNOW WHO ATTENDED YOUR EVENT.** Because my time is limited, I generally send this note via e-mail.
- **SEND A THANK-YOU NOTE TO EVERYONE WHO SIGNED UP FOR YOUR MAILING LIST** and let them know what to expect next; for instance, they'll receive the December issue of your e-zine in the

next week, or they can download their free thank-you e-book for registering via this link.

- **SEND A THANK-YOU NOTE TO EVERYONE WHO PURCHASED SOMETHING FROM YOU.** I love it when people pay me by check because then I can send them a handwritten note thanking them for the purchase. Sounds time-consuming? It is. But it feels so good to know the names and imagine the faces of people who cared enough to purchase (and hopefully read) my book that I like to cement the experience in my memory (and theirs) with a little note of gratitude.

- **CONTINUE TO GENERATE VISIBILITY FOR THE EVENT.** Write about the event on your blog and include photos. Thank everyone who made the event successful, from the organizer and the other readers to the teachers and lecturers, and the folks who came out to support you as listeners.

Speaking to an audience is a dance. Knowing your steps, holding your frame, and trusting when it's time to lead and time to follow will make for a much better experience for you and your listeners, while increasing your odds of meaningful results.

Chapter 19

> THE PRODUCTIVE WRITER PROMOTES EFFECTIVELY BY:
>
> - Having a presence online where you can be easily found.
> - Establishing and nurturing a vibrant social network for communicating and collaborating with people in your field.
> - Reaching out regularly to the audiences who will benefit from what you are offering.
> - Sending respectful, clear messages designed to offer value to the people receiving them.
> - Creating a daily rhythm for moving toward big-picture goals.
> - Having press kit material templates on hand.

If people don't know who you are or what you're doing, they are unlikely to read what you write, hire you, or seek out your expertise. That's why The Productive Writer communicates regularly with interested audiences, clients, prospects, and media to offer them news of her appearances, publications, classes, services, and other offerings.

Many creative writers imagine self-promotion to be an obnoxious bogeyman; they confess this to me under their breath, as if even the word *promotion* were a dirty one. My experience has been the opposite. Self-promotion can be friendly and fun, and it offers a meaningful opportunity to connect with people who are excited about what excites you. It's a way to make the leap from monologue (writing life) to dialogue (public life). And every writer preparing for success has to make that leap at some point. So why not now, on your own terms?

Effective, sustainable promotion happens when you establish foundational systems that can be easily repeated, and then modified over time and for specific purposes. Are you more of a "wizard behind the curtain" type of promoter? No problem. With all of the communication forums available to you in the online world, you can have your quiet, authentic life while simultaneously being in the (virtual) public eye.

Following are the basic tools you'll want to have at your fingertips to make you more visible, more professional, and more memorable.

STOCKING YOUR ARSENAL

Whether you are a creative writer promoting appearances and publications or a business writer promoting your services to potential clients, you'll want to have some basic promotional tools in place and at the ready for when it's time to spread the word. The general idea is that you have a presence online where you can be easily found, a well-established social network for communicating and collaborating with people in your field, and systems in place for reaching the audiences who will benefit from what you are offering. These are today's tools of the trade that can help take you there:

- **FULLY ARTICULATED (AND NAMED) PLATFORM:** See chapter two.
- **WEBSITE:** An online "shingle" where you share your expertise, credentials, services, and offerings. It should give readers an authentic sense of your voice and spirit.
- **BLOG:** A flexible and interactive website that allows you to post regular entries and generate community conversation through comments. You can use a blog as a forum for reinforcing your expertise by sharing your work and wisdom regularly.

- **MAILING LIST:** A list of people who have given you their contact information so you can keep them in the loop about your activities.
- **MEDIA LIST:** Contact information for publications, websites, and blogs that report on your area of expertise. List can be segmented by geography and market type as it grows over time.
- **PRESS KIT:** Described in this chapter on page 193.
- **FACEBOOK:** Connect with colleagues, students, and friends in a social forum where you can share knowledge, resources, offers, and opportunities targeted to the interests and needs of your audience. Your presence here will ideally be integrated both with who you are, your public image as a writer, and your platform(s).
- **TWITTER:** Like Facebook, but in the space of a thimble.
- **LINKEDIN:** Keep your profile current with a résumé and latest accomplishments so colleagues can stay appraised of your experience and expertise. Keep in touch with people and exchange authentic testimonials to help paint a personal picture of your results and spirit. Stay engaged with the changes and successes of peers you would like to continue to work with in the future.

Have these in place? Good! A daily rhythm of just fifteen minutes a day can create a momentum of communication that grows your visibility and your reputation. Concerned about balancing the mix of writing and social media? You should be! Chapter thirteen gives you the reigns so you can put social media to work for you.

GROWING A CONTACT LIST: WHY AND HOW

Your contact list is the lifeblood of your promotion efforts. The more you can keep in touch with people in a way that offers them real value, at reasonable intervals, the more likely you are to establish mutually beneficial long-term relationships. Here some tips for growing yours.

Make It Easy for People to Join

Offer an easy way for folks to sign up to receive information from you online. You can do this on your blog or website with an autoresponder—software that allows you to collect contact information automatically. Viewers will see an invitation to "join my mailing list" and a field for entering their e-mail address; when they do, their information will be added to your contact database. (Autoresponders also make it easy to craft personalized e-mails that look good, and they can be scheduled in advance and measured to see if they're connecting with readers.)

Group Your Contacts by Type of Relationship

General messages about what you're doing may actually hurt your relationships and your image. You may not want to share the news of your story just published in *Mothering* or *Playboy* with your contacts in high-tech marketing departments. And you don't need to alert people who subscribe to your poetry zine (from all over the world) about the marketing copy class you're offering businesses in your hometown.

The simple rule is: Give people what they want, and they're far more likely to stick around. The more specific you can be about what you're saying to whom, the more people are going to pay attention. You can prepare for these relevant communications by developing targeted sublists of contacts that reflect various interest groups. Here are a few examples from my own contact database:

- **SAGE BELIEVERS**: People who know and love me, who don't necessarily give a hoot about the stuff I write about but are happy to hear my good news.
- **CURRENT STUDENTS**: These are grouped by class.
- **PAST STUDENTS**: These are grouped by type of class, so I can continue to send pertinent information to each group about publishing opportunities, inspiring information, and new classes offered.

- **MEDIA (BY LOCALE/REGION):** Contacts to whom I send press releases about events or offerings that are relevant to their audiences.
- **READING SERIES FOLKS:** People who have signed up to receive announcements about the monthly reading series I host.
- **POETRY PEOPLE:** People I know through my poetry teaching, lecturing, and community building—both peers and colleagues.
- **WRITING COLLEAGUES:** These are people in my creative community I exchange wisdom and ideas with.
- **WTLP ZINE:** People who have signed up specifically to receive my free monthly Writing the Life Poetic zine.
- **BIZ COLLEAGUES:** People I work with (and have worked with) in my day job as a marketing communications writer.
- **PROSPECTS:** Any people or organizations I am building relationships with but who are not yet clients or colleagues.

Know why you are communicating with each group and the value you have to offer them. Make sure your message is specific and relevant for readers, providing the information they have requested.

The purpose of communicating with groups of people is to offer something of value that they specifically requested to receive. When you send them this information, they will be reminded of how fabulous you are. And when they next think of [insert your area of passion/expertise here], you will likely come to mind.

If you want them to buy something from you or take some specific action, show them why or how this choice will benefit them. And make it easy for them to do what you are asking.

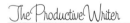

EFFECTIVE COMMUNICATION TO GROUPS

Respecting Privacy

- Always use a bcc function to ensure privacy for group sends. No one appreciates seeing their name on an e-mail that was distributed to eight hundred people. In fact, such a mistake will guarantee people opting out of your list.

- Make sure that there is no way for a recipient to Reply All—ever. Some e-mail group administration services seem to default to this option. I recently experienced absolute anarchy when someone sent a personal note to a musician whose list I subscribe to. This triggered hundreds of angry people in a chain reaction, sending e-mails to the entire list saying they wanted to be removed. You don't want to make your mailing list angry. So don't give subscribers access to each other.

Offering an Opt-Out Option

Not everyone who is on your list today is going to want to hear from you forever. Give people an easy out. If you use an e-mail marketing service like ConstantContact.com, folks can simply use the link at the bottom of every e-mail you send to unsubscribe themselves from your list.

Don't Wear Out Your Welcome

Use restraint when communicating with your peeps. Offer information that is useful, meaningful, timely, informative, or inspiring, and honor any communication time intervals you have promised.

Measure and Modify

If you're using a service like ConstantContact.com, you can track opens and click-throughs for each communication you send. This will help you know what people are responding to and what they're not. You can modify messaging based on the results you're getting.

THE PRESTO PRESS KIT

A press kit is a composite of the information and images you share with the press to make it easy for a journalist to tell your story. You share it when you have something specific and newsworthy to offer, with the intention of having this news made public by someone other than you.

If you have all of the pieces of your press kit in good working order, you can respond to opportunities as they arise. Following are the components I recommend that you develop and make easily accessible:

Press Kit Essentials

- **A PRESS RELEASE TEMPLATE** for telling a particular story that can get versioned per event, location, publication, region, or theme. The main point of the press release is to communicate with clarity: who you are, what you are offering right now, for which audiences, and why those audiences should be excited about it.
- **LATEST BIO.** Includes key publications, recognition, awards, community service, and biographical information that relates to your writing/author identity. Sometimes bios include personal information about the writer's/author's family and where he lives. This is a personal choice. Update regularly either once a month or each time you have a significant change in status to add.
- **PROFESSIONAL AUTHOR PHOTO.** One high-res and one low-res version ready to go.
- **BOOK COVER IMAGE.** One high-res and one low-res version.
- **COPIES (OR CLIPS) OF ALL INTERVIEWS, REVIEWS, FEATURES, AND MENTIONS OF YOU AND YOUR WORK.** Make these available via

links or downloadable PDFs whenever possible, and keep hard-copy clips for publications that prefer this option.

- **SAMPLE(S) OF YOUR WORK.** Keep clips of published pieces of work, both digital and hard copy.
- **ATTRACTIVE FOLDER.** (When sending the press kit via snail mail.)

Nice to Have Someday

- **VIRTUAL INTRODUCTION.** YouTube clips or podcasts featuring you reading, lecturing, teaching, or presenting to an audience.
- **BOOK (OR PROJECT) VIDEO TRAILER.** Give people a multimedia experience of your book and you. This is a fun way to establish a little intrigue about your work and get folks excited to learn more.

To keep things simple you can provide all of media kit components on a single page on your website. This allows you to send a press release in the body of an e-mail, and simply link to your media page for the rest. You should also keep a well-organized supply of hard-copy materials (clips, interviews, and publicity) on hand to include in press kits that you send by snail mail. These will also come in handy if you are applying for grants, scholarships, residencies, or funding.

The Productive Promotion Checklist

As you go, make note of the strategies, materials, and communications that seem most effective, as well as the ones that don't. Note what worked, and how you'll continue this momentum.

 Visit WritersDigest.com/article/productive-writer-downloads for a productive promotion checklist template.

Chapter 20

SKIPPING DOWN THE HILL

YOUR WRITING LIFE IS A LONG-TERM COMMITMENT. IT IS A relationship with yourself and your readers that you very well may be nurturing for the rest of your life. I invite you to think of productivity as the romance that keeps things spicy, surprising, and always evolving. If you get bored with what you are doing, so will everyone else. Productivity means you are always growing toward something specific, with a vision of what waits for you on the other side. And just as in any relationship, there are any number of arrivals and departures. Productivity is the grace with which we navigate these and the creativity with which we adapt to the ever-changing nature of the writing life.

YOUR BODY IS YOUR TEMPLE AND YOUR WORKHORSE

One of the risks of that great discipline of keeping your butt in the chair is the expansion of said butt. Keep in mind that you wouldn't be writing without your body. And it needs you to keep it well fed, exercised, stretched, and rejuvenated so it can show up at your desk every day and do what you ask of it. Plus, if you are like many writers, being physically in motion is one of the best ways to wake up to the interesting ideas and insights that are getting ready to come through.

Consider a regular practice of as many of the following that you have time, interest, and funds for: rigorous walking, massage, yoga,

acupuncture, stretching. Whatever appeals to you and keeps your body feeling like the receptive writing machine you'd like it to be is worth considering, trying, and sustaining for the long term. Because often I'm typing all day and all night, I've to had take extra special care of my arms, hands, back, and neck. One of my favorite (and almost free) rituals is a daily bubble bath with healing herbs and Epsom salts before bed every night. This is my blessed time of giving back to the body that has given so much to me all day long. What is yours?

CELEBRATION IS YOUR BATTLE CRY!

> *My husband once bought a great bottle of wine that we decided to save until I placed my first short story. This was back when we didn't know up from down about storing wine, and by the time the big day came—four or five years later—the wine had turned. Since then I've made it one of my life missions to celebrate everything. Immediately."*

—MONICA WOOD, *author of* The Pocket Muse

Writing is not something we do for or with an audience, a boss, or a team of colleagues. No one is going to pat you on the back after that six-hour shred of a writing session. And no one is going to congratulate you for delivering on your promises to yourself. In short, the only person who has enough information or investment to appreciate how hard you're working is you.

We all know what a difference a little appreciation can make, especially when we are busting our butts (and an occasional button) to accomplish some very strenuous goals.

That's why one of the most important jobs you have as a writer is to celebrate yourself, your successes, your failures, your willingness to take risks, your ability to follow through on your commitments, your capacity to work through fear when it comes up—the whole shebang. Every flawed and magnificent aspect of your writing life deserves to be celebrated each step of the way.

Learning to honor yourself in this way gives you the keys to the Productive Writer kingdom or queendom. When you really start to authentically feel accountable to and appreciated by yourself, it matters less and less what anyone else thinks or believes or says. You become a closed circuit that doesn't depend on any external energy force to make things happen. You transform from a person needing validation to a person deeply secure in who she is and what she is doing. All this from a little celebration. You have it in you, even if it sounds silly. I know you do.

DOCUMENT YOUR SUCCESS

One great way to celebrate is to take a moment or two to document and correctly file every good thing that comes your way in your writing life. I recommend that you create a system of paper or computer files where you record in detail:

- **PUBLICATIONS AND PUBLICITY** (a clip of or link to each one). Log every publication, interview, tip, mention in someone's blog, and review of your work so you can watch your visibility grow. Plus, you'll start to get a sense of who is interested in what you have to say and what their experience of your writing might be. This can help you refine your platform and your approach to productivity as you go.
- **CELEBRATIONS** (a record of good news, good reviews, bad news you handled well, promising rejections, and anything you can possibly count as something to be grateful for). Refer to this

every time you need a shot of faith in yourself—both your accomplishments and your attitude.

- **TESTIMONIALS** (a list of every positive thing said to you by students, editors, clients, colleagues). Attribute each one with a date and context of your relationship with the speaker. These are useful as a pick-me-up for yourself and to share in promotions of all kinds along the way.

TRACK (AND REPEAT) SUCCESS

Try keeping a writing success log to help you track what you're learning. It can also help you stay committed to your own productivity adventure and define success for yourself along the way.

 For a sample Writing Success Log visit
WritersDigest.com/article/productive-writer-downloads.

PREPARE FOR PROSPERITY

The idea that talent and suffering go hand in hand in the writing life has become legendary; the "starving artist" is now an all-too-familiar archetype. I think it's time to blow some kisses to this archetype and bid it adieu. Why? Because it keeps us small, scared, and struggling. And it keeps our writing starved for something bigger in us.

The truth is, starving writers are too busy trying to make ends meet to write much of anything. And the well-fed, reasonably employed writer has such comforts as a roof over her head and some tried-and-true organizational skills to employ toward the success of her writing life—whatever she defines that success to be.

A few years ago, when I had the good fortune to hear Mary Oliver read, she mentioned a review in which the reviewer had no particular objection to Oliver's poetry per se but seemed quite troubled by the fact that this poet found the time to lie around in the grass and con-template nature. Oliver must have a trust fund, the reviewer concluded, in order to afford such leisure, thereby suggesting that poetry is avail-able only to the independently wealthy.

The truth, said Oliver, is that she lives extremely modestly on money she has earned. And in so doing, she is liberated from the over-whelming demands of "making a living" so she has the time and space to make a (writing) life. What Oliver clearly understands (and the reviewer clearly doesn't) is that the wealth of creativity is available to every single one of us in any given moment. We need only choose to tune in wherever we are—whether it be a field of daisies or a swath of concrete—and start writing.

If we don't question the popular paradigm that aligns "wealth" with money, and we make the pursuit of cash a primary goal, we may find that we have little time left over for writing. And on the flip side, if we neglect our material needs in pursuit of a writing life, we are likely to end up in real, uninspiring distress.

But if we agree that a prosperous life is one with time to liter-ally and figuratively smell the roses, and then luxuriate in the time to write about it, we are establishing a root system for a new paradigm of prosperity—one we feed and water with our attention and our words. By recognizing, welcoming, and prioritizing both our material and creative needs, we have a far better chance of striking a balance that feels like true wealth and can sustain us over the long term.

No matter what your financial status, time limitations, or family commitments might be, I know that you have the skills and the cre-ativity to cultivate a spirit and a practice of prosperity both in your life and in your writing. Once you start investigating, you may be sur-prised to find yourself shaping a life that is wealthy with time, inspira-tion, community, and even money. I'll bet you will find yourself doing

more and more of what you love most without sacrificing anything but an old archetype whose time has come and gone.

LET GO AND LET GOOD

Write a list of everything you've been carrying in your writing life that is no longer serving you. Then whittle this list down to only those habits, beliefs, and choices you feel ready to let go of once and for all. Climb to the top of a hill (literal or metaphorical), make a fire, and burn your list. Skip back down the hill, released from who you once were into who you are becoming.

TAKE THE RISK TO BE HAPPY

> *Success is not the key to happiness,*
> *Happiness is the key to success.*
> *If you love what you are doing,*
> *You will be successful."*

–BUDDHA

What's standing between so many of us and our dreams is an idea—conscious or subconscious—that we do not deserve to be successful. The Productive Writer is committed to working through such limiting beliefs because she understands she has important work to do, and she is ready to clear any clutter that's in her way.

It's okay if you're afraid. You can expect to fail; everyone does sooner or later, and the most successful people often fail the most spectacularly. The Productive Writer picks herself up, dusts off her pen and paper, chooses to be grateful for the gifts of wisdom and trust that get cultivated along the path of mistakes and disappointment, and keeps on writing.

WHEN IN DOUBT, WRITE

"What would you do if you could do anything you wanted to?" James Martin, author of *The Jesuit Guide to (Almost) Everything,* asked readers in a recent interview.

When at the Wharton School studying business, this Jesuit priest says he shared his desire to study poetry with his advisor, who responded, "That is the stupidest thing I've ever heard." Martin disagreed, went on to study poetry, and says it's what he remembers best from his education.

Of course, there are dozens of "practical" reasons not to pursue poetry or a writing life of any kind. It's not likely to pay the rent or mortgage, at least for a while, and no one at your job may give a whit about your affinity for Whitman. The good news is this: No one needs to care about the writing you love other than you.

In my experience, when we let love lead, our lives and our work become far less confusing. When we trust our passions to steer us where we are intended to go, we may find ourselves in a less prescribed career track. And it may take some exploring to determine exactly how and where we fit. Good thing creative people are good at exploring!

Inspiration may not immediately fill your bank account, but it is likely to fill your sails. Committing to a productive writing rhythm may not lead to your next big career move. But it just might make you happy. And there's no better compass than happiness.

Who knows, doing exactly what makes us happiest may have an even greater untapped earning potential than that predictable paycheck. With passion as productivity engine, we're far more likely to throw our shoulders into the work and stay with it, simply because it feels better to do so than to stop.

What would you do if you could do anything you wanted to? When in doubt, write.

INDEX

GRATITUDES

A book is a big presence in a family as it takes shape in the margins of a full life. I want to thank my husband, Jonathan Luchs, for his generosity in covering the home bases while I wandered about in the outfield, combing the turf for words and wisdom. Savannah Johnson, beloved friend of our family, has cared for all of us above and beyond the call of duty to allow me the good fortune of writing this book.

I offer my gratitude to Jane Friedman and Kelly Nickel at Writer's Digest Books for welcoming me back into the fold, to my editor Scott Francis for his diligent and insightful guidance, delivered with the loveliest of accents. I sleep better at night thanks to my agent Rita Rosenkranz's savvy oversight of this project. And I owe a special debt to the Productive Writers who have offered their hard-earned wisdom and success strategies quoted throughout this book.

Writers in my local and extended community have humbled me with their generosity, uplifted me with their talent and wisdom, and offered an alchemy of grace through their friendship. My students around the world have taught me so much about what is possible in the life poetic. And at the foundation of every good thing in my life is the root system of dear friends and family who have laughed, cried, and paraded with me through the years. I offer special thanks to my parents, Bobbi Cohen and Bryan Cohen, for demanding excellence, reflecting and honoring what is best in me, and for the foundation of creativity and hard work that has sourced my own.

Most importantly, I thank you, dear reader, for honoring your call to write, and for your courage to aspire to the best that you and your writing can be.